NAOMI MITCHISON, distinguished novelist, journalist, and social critic, has a list of publications to her name that span over forty years of varied literary, administrative, and political activity. Some of her best-known books are *Cloud Cuckoo Land, The Moral Basis of Politics,* and *The Bull Calves,* as well as several books for young readers. She is the daughter of J. S. Haldane and the sister of J. B. S. Haldane, both distinguished British scientists. Mrs. Mitchison's husband is the Labour M.P. for Kettering.

"I have written all my life," says Mrs. Mitchison, "and can't stop. I also run a farm [in Argyll, Scotland], a large house, and have a kind of extended family including twenty grandchildren. However, this is only the beginning. In Botswana I have been accepted by the Bakgatla, a tribe of some 30,000 people. I try to be their mother and counselor, to help them in every way, as a tribeswoman should help her fellows. I get plenty in return, perhaps less tangible but fully as valuable."

AFRICAN HEROES

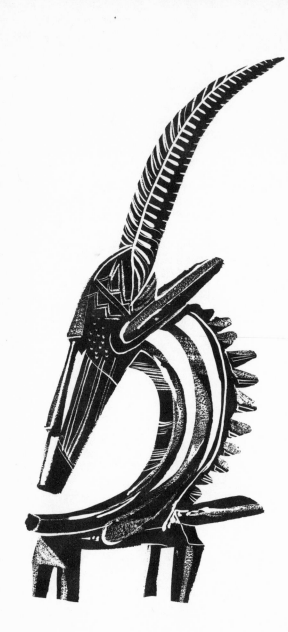

Illustrated by William Stobbs

Naomi Mitchison

AFRICAN HEROES

Farrar, Straus & Giroux   New York
An Ariel Book

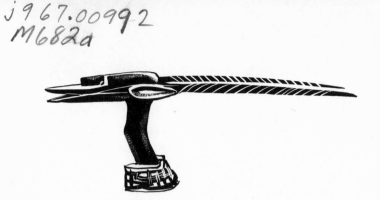

Author's Note

Why write this book? Well, during the last five years I have become deeply involved with Africa. I have dear friends there, whom I love and trust even if they don't write to me; I know when I go back that past and future will join up happily, African fashion, into the present. I pay tax in Mochudi, the capital of my tribe; I am irrevocably a Mokgatla—that is one of the Kgatla people—and because of that I count myself *de facto*, if not *de jure*, a Motswana. This means I have obligations and loyalties to my little, struggling country of Botswana, and above all to my own tribe, which may sometimes, in some ways, conflict with my loyalties as a British citizen. But it also means, I think, that I have learned to slip into an African skin, to think and feel as an African, to have it said to me lovingly: "I cannot think of you as white." Yet, remember, all writers are shape changers or, if you like, so strung that they can play tunes in all modes. The ancients knew this, honoring their bards or *griots* or prophets, expecting them to tell the truth about situations into which ordinary people were too hurried or scared to enter. Perhaps we are all one.

You see, I am playing an African tune and, doing that, I try to be the same kind of person as the tellers of these stories, all of which stayed in the minds and mouths of the people who told them, from one generation to the next. For most of them I have had to go to written sources, but some, especially perhaps the stories of Shaka and Moshesh, were written by people who had themselves listened to the tellers of history. Still, I have tried to keep the flavor and rhythm of the spoken word. One way I know what that is, in my own mind, is because of all the evenings I have spent with our tribal historian and senior uncle, Amos Kgaman-yane Pilane, whom I speak of on page 142.

How often I have walked over from the chief's house on the hill, where I live myself, cutting across the dry stream bed, past the thatched houses, where people wave and greet me, past the big tree and across the sandy, prickly waste ground where the children play and the goats pick at whatever they can find, and so to Amos's *lapa*, the low walls glowing in the sunset. He will be sitting on the step of his house, perhaps with a favorite grandson in his arms. But if it is already late and a hot summer night, the grand-children will be asleep on their mats in the *lapa*, the little courtyard, their brown, soft bodies slack and lovely in the moonlight.

Then Amos will begin to tell me the story of my tribe and of other African tribes, speaking slowly, using rather long words, often from the Bible, not letting me interrupt. Perhaps we share supper, a bowl of porridge, and, if we are lucky, a cup of sour milk, and he lays his wisdom before me until I walk back, late and safe, through Mochudi, past the evening fires and the singing that goes on half the night.

So, through him and through my Chief, Kgosi Linchwe II, who is now Botswana's ambassador in Washington, and through a dozen other friends, I was able to slip into feeling African. And this led me to realize that here were people whose heroes had been taken from them, and led me further to think what the white invaders had done over six centuries or so of African history, not only to the bodies of Africans but to their minds. It is bad for people to have their heroes taken away from them, even if the heroes were, like most of the heroes in early European history, war leaders and believers in the strong arm. And perhaps it is equally bad for the invaders to be able to look down on the invaded as people without culture and without a heroic past. If this book had gone on into modern times, we might have had such heroes as John Chilembwe, Chief Luthuli, and some who are not dead but who are held in prison, Mandela, Sisulu, Sobukwe, and others, and with them at least one white man who is also an African hero: Bram Fischer. May it not be the end for them!

Contents

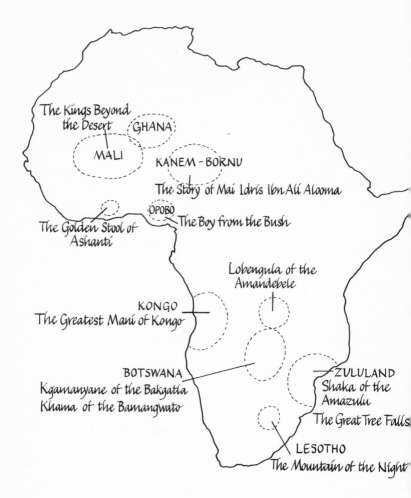

The Kings Beyond
the Desert

GHANA

MALI

KANEM - BORNU

The Story of Mai Idris Ibn Ali Alooma

OPOBO

The Golden Stool of
Ashanti

The Boy from the Bush

Lobengula of the
Amandebele

KONGO
The Greatest Mani of Kongo

BOTSWANA
Kgamanyane of the Bakgatla
Khama of the Bamangwato

ZULULAND
Shaka of the
Amazulu

The Great Tree Falls

LESOTHO
The Mountain of the Night

Map 1
The areas in which the stories
in this book take place

Map 2
The political boundaries of
modern Africa

AFRICAN HEROES

1 The Kings Beyond the Desert

At the northern end of the long trade route was the glitter of the blue Mediterranean, the Middle Sea, and the marvelous Saracen seaports: Tripoli, Tunis, Algiers, and Safi. Here all traded and the honest traders hated the pirates, Christian or Moslem. Men came for trade from the far north, from the courts of the Angevin Kings of England or the rulers of the Holy Roman Empire; from the Sultans of the East and the High Kings of Ireland. They brought the goods of their own country: well-woven woolen cloth from England and the Low Countries, furs of sable and miniver from Tartary, wheat from whichever of the northern countries had been blessed with a good harvest. Or they brought precious stones from India and porcelain from China by way of Southeast Asia. Trade went on in all the streets and markets of the great cities. Men bought and sold marbles and tiles for buildings. They bought exquisite handwritten manuscripts for scholars. They bought scents and tortoiseshell and dragon's blood from the land of Zanj. They bought carved work and glasswork, enamel work from Burgundy, marvelously engraved elephant ivory from Ceylon, where so many pilgrims visited the mountain shrine of Adam's Foot, or the walrus-ivory chessmen from Iceland, which also sent the great white pelts of the unbelievable ice bears. There was wine—but not for good Moslems—and all kinds of spices and scented oils and delicious food. There were slaves, black or brown mostly, and often, besides those, captives held for ransom. Oh, they were wonderful cities, these seaports of the Saracens!

And if traders went south with a train of loaded camels? They would need to take a good guide who would lead from one water hole to another, for it might be three days between them. The camels could manage, but by the end of a long route they were thin and exhausted and must be fed again. South they went under the sun and the camel riders ate meagerly, dates and thin rounds of bread baked on the cooking stones.

Beyond the mountains, a month's journey from the western coast, but three months and maybe more from the cities of the north, lay the oasis and city of Audoghast. It was so rich that the young women would not soil their hands with any kind of work but thought only of their beauty and their fair skins, never exposed to harsh sunlight, and the old men cared only for the pleasures and

4

surprises of good cookery. There was so much water they could grow all kinds of fruit and crops, and to this city too merchants came from all parts. The last days before getting there were the worst and the caravans used to send a messenger ahead to Audoghast, so that water could be brought out to them. There was much gold here, but it came from the southern land of Ghana or even from south of Ghana, from the dark forests full of devils. But the nearer you got to its sources, the better trade you could do; the caravans moved on.

So again the camels rested and watered and marched on over the sand waves of the desert, marked here and there by the bones of the beasts or slaves who had fallen by the thirsty way. Day after day, and still the caravans must go on and ever on, south toward the gold. The merchants covered their heads and faces, but the blown dust pitted their skins. Only the thought of gold carried them on. But at last the desert seemed to be ending. There were more bushes; the camels could snatch a bite here and there. And so they came to the cities of the Africans and the places set aside for merchants from the north where the camels could rest and the bales of goods could be put into safety. Some of the merchants would find other Moslems who would give them hospitality; they or their fathers would have come from the north, though most had married African wives. But a few would have the blue eyes and light-brown skin of the Berber people from the hills a little way from the Mediterranean coast.

The earliest merchants came to a state called Ghana, with a capital that was called Kumbi; really it was two capitals a few miles apart. One was the Moslem capital, where the merchants lodged. Here there were mosques and schools and gatherings of learned Imams. Here there was stone, carved and jointed. But the other was where the pagan King of Ghana held his court and here in the sacred groves around the city of low thatched houses were the terrible shrines of the African gods where sacrifices too dreadful to think about were carried out and where drums buzzed and thudded like a fevered pulse all night.

At the King's court the hounds wore collars and bells of gold and silver; the bits and buckles of the horses' bridles were pure gold and so were the peaks of the saddles; the saddlecloths were sewn and edged with gold and held with gold bosses. All men wore gold, pages and counselors and vassals; the King of Ghana wore gold wherever he could carry it. There was much bowing and bustling. The court musicians would play on stringed instruments and sing songs of praise. Many of the King's court would be long-robed Moslems and speech would be courteous and lengthy. There would be exchange of gifts and news and compliments. But in time the merchants could spread out their wares, laying the bales all around the courtyard of the King. And gold would be bought. Gold, gold. The golden nuggets would be weighed and wrapped. There would be bargaining. But here in Ghana there was so much gold and the merchants who had come so far, braving the desert, set out again for the north and the cities of the coast with unbelievable riches.

Yet not one of these merchants from the north came near the place where the gold was mined along the banks of the great rivers. That was still farther south under the dark arches of the great forests where elephants and lions and leopards ruled over men. Here those from Ghana brought merchandise, beads and salt mostly, and laid it on the banks of the rivers. When they had withdrawn out of sight, the naked, black-skinned miners came and laid down nuggets of gold or calabashes full of gold dust beside the merchandise, and in this way the trade was made with no words spoken.

It was not always to Ghana that the merchants came and it was not always gold they brought back. Sometimes they brought slaves, prisoners taken from the southern people either in war or trapped like forest beasts to sell— men, women, and children. They were worth good money in the seaports, where they would be sold again, and would have to spend all their lives working for masters who might be kind or might be unkind but whose language they could not understand. And they would never see their homes again, for how could they ever come back across the terrible deserts? But for the merchants they were only something to buy at one price and sell for perhaps twice or three times as much.

As for Ghana, the day came when the city of Kumbi was destroyed and new names were spoken of in the Saracen trading cities. The next merchants took their caravans along the same desert routes, but now to Mali. And again this was a country whose African rulers were Moslem or at least part Moslem, though they ruled over pagans or part pagans. And this state and its courts, like Ghana before it, was founded on gold.

The royal family of Mali, the Keitas, were Mandingo, tall and splendid and glistening black. They were Moslems, but they also served other deities if the need arose,

7

and the *jinns,* who are Moslem spirits, would be invoked to help them. They were great hunters and knew the secrets of the Bush. They had been kings for many generations; for first they had been village chiefs, then tribal chiefs and at last they were called Mansa, which has the meaning of King over other Kings. There was one of these kings called Maghan Kon Fatta, Maghan the handsome; his clan came from a lion, and lion-like they were in war. He had a beautiful wife, Sassouma Berété, who had borne him a handsome son and daughter. But one day two hunters came to his court with a strange tale and a still stranger young girl with them, ugly as a hippopotamus, with a hump on her back.

They told the King how they had magically killed the terrible buffalo of Do which was ravaging the countryside, and how the King of Do had given them their choice of all the maidens. But the old woman who had told them the spell with which to take the power from the buffalo had bidden them choose the ugliest girl, for she was the spirit of the buffalo, as also she was the spirit of that same old woman whose ancestor had been a buffalo. They brought this girl to King Maghan and he, warned by prophecies, said he would wed her. The girl was called Sogolon Kedjou, and she was strange and terribly strong like a buffalo. But in spite of her looks the King loved her, and in time she bore him a son. Now the King's *griot,* the poet who was always with him, who was historian and counselor, rememberer of the past and the one most able to see into the future, knew that this son would somehow be a great king, as great as Alexander the Two-Horned, the Greek who conquered all the world as far as India.

This *griot*, whose name was Gnankouman Doua, immediately made a song of welcome to the babe who was both lion and buffalo, and it was he who cried out the name Mari Djata, which the child was to have. But he was called by his mother's name, Sogolon Djata, and that, in the quick Mandingo speech, became Sundiata, and that is his hero name.

Now this child, born with such good omens, with poets and poetesses vying with one another to celebrate him, was a sickly child, with a head too big for his shoulders. He did not speak and he did not walk. And Sassouma Berété, whose son was growing into a fine lad, mocked at Sogolon, who tried everything to get her son to walk. But it was no use. She bore the King a daughter called Kolonkan, but she was almost as ugly as her mother; at that, King Maghan sent Sogolon and her family to live in the back part of the great household. He himself married the beautiful Princess Namandje, and when she bore him a son, the soothsayers said that he would grow up to be the best friend of a great king. But who would be the great king? Surely not this crawling child!

Yet one day King Maghan made the child Sundiata come to him and told him that now he was going to pass on to him the present which every king must give to his heir. Gnankouman Doua had been his *griot*, as his father had been the *griot* of King Maghan's father. "And now," said the King, "the son of Doua, Balla Fasséké, will be your *griot*. From his mouth you will hear the history of your ancestors and you will learn the art of governing Mali according to their principles. Be inseparable friends from now on with Balla Fasséké. May your destiny be accomplished; never forget that Niani is your capital and Mali the cradle of your ancestors."

And then the child, who had been sitting on a skin rug at his father's feet, silent as always, called to Balla to come and sit on the skin beside him. "You will be my *griot*," he said, for he had understood all.

But soon afterward the King died, and the Council, paying no attention to his wishes or the words of Gnankouman Doua, passed over the crawling child and made Sassouma Bérété's son King. Sogolon was mocked at, and her son Sundiata looked sullen and fierce. They had a little vegetable garden where Sogolon worked, the tears running down her cheeks, the babies beside her. And then suddenly Sundiata saw how his mother was suffering and made up his mind to walk. Balka Fasséké did his bidding and went to the royal smith, who, like many smiths, was a soothsayer. He knew what the young *griot* wanted and sent six of his apprentices to Sogolon's hut, carrying the iron bar which had been made and kept for this day. The boy crawled toward it, took it in one hand, stood it on the ground, and then heaved himself to his feet.

But the tremendous bar was bent into a bow. Balla Fasséké began the song that was to echo through Mali:

> "Take your bow, hunter.
> Take your bow, Sogolon Djata!"

From that day onward Sundiata walked. Now his mother was no longer mocked. The young princes from other kingdoms who were being brought up at the court of Mali came and played with him, but his best friend was Manding Bory, son of the beautiful Queen Namandje. When she

10

died, Manding Bory was brought up by Sogolon as her own son. Balla Fasséké, a little older than they were, taught them and sang to them and brought them up in the ways of goodness.

But the Queen Mother, Sassouma Berété, was more jealous than ever. How could she get rid of Sundiata? She called together the nine witches of Mali and gave them handsome presents, telling them what must be done. The witches were reluctant to turn their fatal powers onto one who had never harmed them, but Sassouma Berété advised them to go to Sogolon's vegetable patch and pick some of the best herbs. "Sundiata is mean and greedy," she said. "He will beat you, old as you are. Then you will have some reason to hate him."

So this was agreed on and the next evening the boy Sundiata and his friends came back from hunting to find the nine bent old witches in his mother's garden, stealing the choicest of the leaves. They pretended to run away, thinking he would catch them, but he was only sorry for them. "Stop, stop," he said. "Don't run away, poor old women! You shall have what you want." And he and his friends, the young princes, filled the old women's baskets with herbs and onions.

Then the oldest witch said, "Listen, Sundiata. This was a test. We were sent here by the Queen Mother to make you behave badly and so draw the powers of evil down onto you. But nothing will hurt a heart full of kindness. Forgive us now."

"I forgive you," said Sundiata. "And we will give you meat from our hunting. We will give you an elephant each!"

So they smiled, saying, "Thank you, son of Justice. From now on, we will watch over you."

Thus the plot against Sundiata came to nothing, and by this time Sundiata had learned many of the mysteries of sorcery, for it is well for a king to know them. And there were two others who were watching over him without his knowledge, his sister Sogolon Kolonkan and his half sister, Nana Triban, the daughter of Sassouma Berété, but how different from her mother!

Yet there was always danger. Sogolon decided that they must all leave the country and go far, far away. Later they would come back, for Sundiata's destiny must be fulfilled. But the young King, Dankara Touman, who was still under the thumb of his mother, sent Balla Fasséké as the head of an embassy to the King of the Susu, Soumaoro Kante; he had no right to do this, as Balla Fasséké was Sundiata's own *griot*, given to him by his father. Sundiata was deeply angry, but he could do nothing. The Susu, who lived to the north of Mali, nearer to the great desert, were a powerful tribe whose King had begun to think of new conquests. And indeed it was they who had helped to destroy the empire of Ghana, eating into it year after year and demanding tribute. Now King Soumaoro was beginning to turn his eyes to Mali, and he held Balla Fasséké as his prisoner.

The first place where Sogolon and her children stayed was at the court of the sorcerer king, Mansa Konkon; the king's children and Sundiata with his half brother, Manding Bory, and his two sisters, Kolonkan and the little Djamarou, played together and were well received. But after two months the old sorcerer sent for eleven-year-old Sun-

12

diata and asked him to play a game of *worri*, which is something like a very fast kind of draughts. "And what will be the stakes?" said Sundiata boldly.

"If I win—and I shall certainly win—I shall kill you."

"And if I win?"

"I shall give you anything you ask for. But I always win."

So while he was playing the first deal, King Konkon sang the song of winning. But when he was playing, Sundiata sang the same song, only he put in new words:

> "Once guests were sacred,
> But the gold came yesterday!"

And then King Konkon started up in anger, throwing down the *worri* board. "Someone has betrayed me!" he shouted. For the wicked Sassouma Bereté had sent him gold only the day before, with a request to get rid of Sundiata. He threw away the *worri* board angrily, but told Sundiata that he and his family must leave at once.

Their next stopping place was Tabon, the mountain city with iron gates, whose prince, Fran Kamara, had been one of Sundiata's playmates and a pupil of his *griot*. But his father was anxious not to be involved in a quarrel with the ruler of Niani and Mali and advised them to go on with the next caravan toward the north. But Fran Kamara swore to be true to his old friend and, when he became king, to help him with all his warriors.

Now they set off by camel for Ghana, and for Wogadou, its main city, which had replaced Kumbi now that so much of the old empire had been eaten up by the Susu and by Soumaoro, the rich and cruel King who still kept Balla Fasséké prisoner. At first Sogolon and the children were wary of the camels, which they had never seen before, but they got used to them. Here in the north there were more camels, and also more horses, many of them very beautiful and highly trained horses from Arabia with richly decorated bridles and saddles.

At Wogadou they found very few people who spoke the Mandingo tongue, and they also saw many traders from the north with their pale faces and curious-colored eyes. However, they soon found an interpreter and were presented to the King of Ghana, who received them kindly, all the time watching the boy Sundiata, who was looking around him, but not childishly, rather as a brave envoy from another land. The family were given lodgings in the palace; Sogolon was very weary after her journey, but the children were happy and treated as sons by the King of Ghana. A year later they moved on again, this time to Mema, far to the east in the lands of the Niger, which was ruled by the King's cousin.

Young Sundiata was constantly with the leader of the caravans, and while they encamped at night under the great arch of stars, with the fires alight and the sweetmeats being passed around, the leader would tell him of the far lands, of Mecca itself, to which one of Sundiata's ancestors had made the pilgrimage, and the country of Alexander the Great. He spoke of Egypt and the pyramids, of how the divine Nile rose and watered the land every year without fail. And, being a good Moslem, he saw to it that Sundiata and Manding Bory prostrated themselves duly in prayer.

At Mema the King's sister received Sogolon and the family with great affection and respect. Here the boys went hunting again and, a little later, went with the King on a campaign against the mountain people, where Sundiata, now fifteen years old, distinguished himself by his courage and strength and intelligence. The King of Mema took him in his arms and thanked him. In another three years the King had decided that this young man must be his successor and viceroy, governing Mema while he was away, for he had no sons of his own. But Sogolon always told her son not to think that his destiny was here in the north. One day he must go back to Mali and be acknowledged Mansa in the city of Niani.

How often Sundiata thought of his *griot*, Balla Fasséké, and wondered whether he had come back from his embassy to King Soumaoro of the Susu and when they would meet again! For now it was more than seven years since they had seen one another. But what had happened there? The sorcerer King of Susu, descendant of smiths, masters of fire, had so terrified all the neighboring kings that they submitted to him, and this included the young King of Mali, Dankara Touman, the son of the wicked queen. Indeed, he was so afraid that he sent his sister, Nana Triban, to be a wife to the sorcerer, and she went in tears.

The King lived in a high tower; up long ladders, guarded by many doors, was the room of enchantments. Nobody but the King dared to go there. But Balla Fasséké had his own magic to protect him; he climbed the ladders, he pushed past the curtains; he came to the room where King Soumaoro kept the sources of his power, the shapes of wood and metal, the masks and pots. Hung on the walls were human skins, and one was on the King's seat. There were serpents and owls and curved swords; there were the watching skulls of murdered kings; all came quiveringly to life when Balla Fasséké came in but he calmed them by his own magic and looked about him. There by the door was a beautiful and enormous *balafon,* the instrument which is played with little hammers; he was overcome with the need to play on it, and it had the most beautiful tone of any instrument he had ever handled. As he played, everything seemed to listen. Human skulls grew eyes and ears to hear him; the owls swayed above the bed. But the *balafon* also called to its master, the sorcerer, and in a moment King Soumaoro plunged into the room with his sword drawn.

Balla Fasséké did not blanch; instead he began a new song on the *balafon:*

"Hail hunter of the deadly arrow
Who shot kings and skinned them,
Who used their skins for clothing,
Who sits on human skins!"

And King Soumaoro paused and listened, as the rest of the room had done, to the beautiful notes of the *balafon* and the beautiful voice of Balla Fasséké. At last he said: "Balla Fasséké, you must say goodbye forever to Mali. You are my *griot* now." And this was the final thing which meant war between Sundiata and Soumaoro Kante, the sorcerer king, who cared nothing for the word of Allah.

But Soumaoro in his wickedness pulled down a tree, which fell on his head. He was one who constantly carried

16

off women, wives or maidens, and locked them up for his own evil purposes. And at last he carried off Keleya of the Magic Cooking Pots, the wife of his nephew Fakoli. Fakoli, with his own tribe, marched out of the Susu country and called for all the kings who had been oppressed by his uncle to come and join him. Even King Dankara Touman declared war, but when he was attacked by the armies of Susu, he fled far south into the forest and was heard of no more. Soumaoro took his revenge by burning the town of Niani and proclaiming himself King of Mali.

But the people of Mali hated him, and the soothsayers said with one voice that the rightful heir to the throne, Sogolon's son, must be found and brought back to rescue Mali. So a search party was sent to find Sundiata, among them a clever and knowledgeable woman called Magnouma. They left Mali and went east and north.

Sundiata's sister Kolonkan was doing the marketing for his mother, who was growing old and feeble. She went to market at Mema with her ladies-in-waiting, and saw a woman selling sweet leaves and flavoring herbs which nobody else had. Kolonkan picked them up and crumbled them between her fingers, sniffing at them.

"Do you wish for these, lady?" said the woman, who was no other than Magnouma. "Nobody in Mema wants them."

"But I am from Mali," said Kolonkan. "We used to have a vegetable garden ourselves. My brother used to guard it."

"And your brother's name, lady?"

"His name is Sogolon Djata and I am Sogolon Kolonkan."

So now one of the men came up, also pretending to be a merchant, and asked if they could visit the lady's mother. So it was arranged. How happy Sogolon was to hear of visitors from Mali! She had food and soft cushions made ready for them. They came, and lo, they were the high ones from her husband's court, whom she remembered of old, including even a brother of Queen Sassouma, who was as anxious as the rest to get back the rightful heir! They thanked God first, that He had brought them to the right place, and then gave news of Mali and the disasters which had overtaken the country. When they spoke of the conquest and burning of Niani, Sundiata grew very angry. And at last they said to him: "Your throne waits for you, Sundiata. Come! Mali is saved because we found you."

"I will come," said Sundiata. "The time for words is past." And he strode out to speak to the King of Mema. All was made ready. But his mother, Sogolon, the buffalo woman, having seen his destiny about to be fulfilled, lay down and died, and was buried with all royal honors. The King of Mema was grieved and angry, but who can stand against one who is both lion and buffalo? In the end he gave Sundiata half his army, cavalry armed with iron swords and lances on beautiful horses. Manding Bory, now fifteen years old, rode beside his half brother, and the two girls, his sisters, also came with the army. At Woga-dou also the King gave him half the Ghanaian army, to avenge the wrongs which the Susu had done to Ghana.

Next, Sundiata turned toward Tabon, where his old playmate Fran Kamara was now King. On his way he met the Susu army ranged across the valley which led to Ta-bon; it was usual to wait for dawn before engaging in battle, but Sundiata was so angry that he charged them at once, and his cavalry tore through the infantry of Susu. This first defeat of Soumaoro's army put heart into all the allies. The savior of Mali was indeed returning!

At the next battle, Sundiata had more troops, for he had been joined by Fran Kamara with all his tribe. They fought a pitched battle at Wegueboria, but whenever Sundiata followed the sorcerer king and was at last about to strike him, lo and behold, Soumaoro was on the next hill! How was such an enemy to be dealt with? At another battle many of Sundiata's men were killed or thrown into panic. This was strong sorcery and Sundiata was angry and uncertain.

Yet more and more kings and chiefs came to join Sundiata, their soldiers armed with spears and bows and swords. Would they be strong enough to defeat King Soumaoro, who also had raised more troops and was about to come back and attack? How did one deal with so strong a sorcerer?

The answer came, at the very moment when Sundiata, on the advice of the most famous soothsayers in Mali, was making a great sacrifice. Balla Fasséké and Nana Triban had escaped from the locked and dreadful house of the sorcerer and had arrived at last. What greetings were there! Princess Nana Triban wept for joy, remembering the crippled child, her half brother, whom she had played with and loved, and now here was the splendid avenger! She told Sundiata how she had been forced to become the wife of Soumaoro, but she had always thought that one day she would find the secret of his power and so escape. She was as clever as she was beautiful, so she became

Soumaoro's favorite and pretended that she was only interested in furthering his cause; he did not know that everything she heard from him was passed on secretly to Balla Fasséké, nor did Balla Fasséké let the sorcerer guess that he was anything but his faithful *griot*.

And then she told her brother how she had been to the magic chamber and had found out that the one thing which could pierce the magician to the heart was the spur of a white cock. Gladly Sundiata heard her and lovingly thanked her. Manding Bory got ready for him an arrow tipped with a cock's spur for the morrow's battle.

But before the battle Balla Fasséké, once more the *griot* of Sundiata, praised all the chiefs and kings who had come to join his royal master, and most of all Sundiata himself, son of the buffalo, protector of the innocent. "Mali, open Mali of the wide plains, is the bright country; in the south under the dreadful forest trees it is dark. But here we need shining words and deeds, the words from the *griots* and the deeds from the warriors. Go forward then, Sundiata, to the plain of Krina, and lay the tyrant low!"

The next morning both armies were ready. Sundiata charged at the head of his cavalry; the horses reared and fought one another with their fore hoofs. All across the field there was terrible fighting. From the tents Sundiata's sisters watched, but none more eagerly than Nana Triban, his half sister, who had armed him with the one weapon that could destroy the sorcerer. Sundiata looked everywhere for Soumaoro and at last found him; he shot with the wooden arrow, and the cock's spur grazed the sorcerer on the shoulder. But through that tiny wound all his powers rushed out; he trembled; a great black bird flew across the sun. He let out a mournful cry and fled from the battlefield. Seeing him in flight, his armies broke and scattered in all directions. Only his son, Susu Balla, stayed with the King of Susu. Sundiata and the nephew Fakoli, whose wife had been stolen, followed him hard. He vanished into a mountain cave, but Fakoli had captured Susu Balla, the son.

And now Sundiata attacked Soumaoro's city of Susu, the walled city with the magician's tower high above everything. The gates were stormed, the houses were set on fire. Sweeping everything before him, Sundiata came to the palace; Balla Fasséké, who knew it well, took him up to the chamber of magic. But here everything was dying; the owls had fallen from their perch, the snakes hung limp. A wind was blowing away the human skins. Down below waited the wives of Soumaoro, the captive princesses, all hoping for a deliverer. And Sundiata destroyed Susu utterly, just as Soumaoro had destroyed Niani. Nothing was left to show where it had been.

Now Sundiata rode from city to city. If their kings had not already acknowledged him, now was the time. Balla Fasséké rode with him in the full dress of the greatest of *griots*. Sundiata sent back an embassy to Mema with gifts of all kinds, saying that they should be allies forever. And at last came the day of triumph, when all were gathered together and peace was declared among all the peoples. Then the kings brought their great iron-headed spears and plunged them into the ground in front of Sundiata, acclaiming him Mansa. The drums repeated it, then the dancers. Even the horses danced before Sundiata. The prisoners, among them Susu Balla, were driven out in front of the armies; most would be sold as slaves. Then Sundiata returned their spears to the kings who had thrust them into the ground, swearing eternal brotherhood, and most of all to Fran Kamara, his old playmate, whose children and children's children would be brought up with his own.

Now after this there was peace in Mali and the city of Niani was rebuilt. Mansa Sundiata had no more need to lead his armies to war, though they kept the boundaries of his kingdom secure. All went well. With the help of his counselors and his *griot* he made good laws; justice prevailed everywhere and prosperity increased. His sisters married noble husbands. Gold from farther south, from the dark forests, began to flow steadily into the Bright Country of Mali; the merchants from the north came more often.

He married beautiful wives who were like sisters to one another, and he built himself a palace and planted trees and scented flower bushes in and around it.

A traveler from the north described that palace. In the outer court Sundiata made a platform of three steps with a carpet of woven silk which had been brought from the eastern lands by camel and cost almost its weight in gold. There were cushions of silk stuffed thickly with the softest feathers. Above all was spread the royal umbrella topped by a golden falcon, and here it was that Sundiata sat and did justice among his counselors and captains. He was surrounded by poets and musicians and beautiful dark girls, his daughters and the daughters of his counselors, with gold and silver circlets on their heads, naked and lovely or wearings beads around their necks and loins. His armor bearers carried gold and silver lances, swords ornamented with gold, with golden scabbards and tassels, quivers for arrows of gold and silver, and gold-set crystal maces. Sometimes jugglers tossed and caught the golden swords.

But the poets were the strangest, for they were masked as birds with cloaks of bird feathers. They sang and shouted the praises of Sundiata and his ancestors and in the end the chief poet mounted the steps of the platform and laid his head in Mansa Sundiata's lap. Then, stepping to the top of the platform, he laid his head first on Sundiata's right shoulder and then on his left, speaking all the while very quickly in the language of Mali and tossing his beaked mask. Was the chief poet the *griot,* Balla Fasseke? Did he sometimes wear this strange disguise? It is possible. For such customs were old, from before Islam, when the far-back ancestors of the Mandingoes were fighting their way to power. But Sundiata knew that without the past there is no future, and without the ancestors the children and grandchildren cannot do great deeds.

If any of his subjects were summoned or came before him for justice or reward, they would wear old clothes and crawl on the ground, then stand bowed and silent. But if King Sundiata deigned to speak to him, the man would joyfully throw dust over his head and shoulders.

Thus Mansa Sundiata lived in peace and wisdom and wealth while the armies, which as a young man he had led, kept his frontiers and suppressed rebellions and sold the prisoners as slaves. And in time he went to join his forefathers and the company of the dead, and the poets sang songs about him to his son who reigned after him, and after his son his grandson, Mansa Musa, who also was a great King of Mali.

In Mansa Musa's time Mali was the most orderly and peaceable of countries. The merchants who came to trade knew that their goods and their persons were utterly safe. Even if they happened to die in Mali, their possessions would be carefully kept and returned to their heirs. And the gold flowed in. Only the country of Songhai, north and east beyond old Ghana and a bend in the river Niger, and stretching for hundreds and thousands of miles along the trading routes, had as much gold at Mali. Mansa Musa looked frowningly at Songhai and spoke of it to his captains. But for himself it seemed to him most needful that after ruling and fighting for seventeen years he should make the *Hadj*, the pilgrimage to Mecca, which all true Moslems should make if it is in any way possible for them. He would need to be away from his kingdom for many months, perhaps for years. There was weeping among his wives, but they knew that when a man's mind was set on pilgrimage, even the most beautiful woman in the world could not turn him.

He would not go on pilgrimage alone. He had an army of followers, but a peaceful army. From his own immediate household he took five hundred strong and handsome slaves, each carrying a golden wand. There were also many others, all Moslems, who perhaps without the generosity of their king would never have been able to make the great pilgrimage. Most of them were black-skinned Mandingoes or Susu, but Mansa Musa himself was lighter in color, although certainly no Arab or Berber. He was purely an African of Africa. Mansa Musa was a man of a most serious mind, one to whom prayer meant much, nor was he ever known to break any one of the rules which bind a good Moslem to the life which the Prophet has laid down for him.

After many days he and his camels and horsemen, traveling north and then east by Walata and Tuat, came to the coast of the blue Mediterranean, its waters stretching on and on! All those strange people with light eyes and yellow hair like sheep! You went down to the edge of the water and it broke and hissed at you, trying to chase you up the sand. But when you were used to that and stooped to touch it, the water was salt, you could not drink it. And it was on this that the ships swayed up and down, bigger than houses.

It may be that some of Mansa Musa's followers went by ship, but that might have been dangerous because of the pirates who would surely have tried to seize his huge hoards of gold, which would have been much spoken about. It is more likely that he remade his caravan and went east by land. It may be indeed that he never reached a Saracen trading city. That does not come into the story. But when at last he came to Egypt it is known that Mansa Musa waited on the Turkish Sultan El-Malik en-Nisian. And the Sultan bade his governors and servants see that all went well with the pilgrims from Africa, who were so good-natured and perhaps overtrustful, thinking all men were as honest as themselves, something indeed laughable for the shopkeepers of Cairo. All honor was given to the King of Mali by the Sultan and he in return showed himself generous to all, so generous indeed that when at last he came back from the Holy Places he had made so many charitable gifts and had built so fine a hostel for future pilgrims from Mali that he had no money left.

But there were plenty willing to help so rich and noble a monarch and it was known that the Negroes beyond the desert always kept their word. One merchant of Alexandria rode back with Mansa Musa to have his loan repaid, but himself died in Timbuktu, which by now was a noble Moslem city with many fine schools and mosques. No matter. Mansa Musa saw to it that his heirs were repaid.

Among those who rode back with him was a poet from Granada in Moorish Spain. They had met in Mecca and Mansa Musa loved him at once. "Will you come back with me," he asked, "and write about my country and my court? I will fill the lap of your robe with gold."

And the poet, who was called El Saheli, felt as poets do, that he must by all means say yes to a new and beautiful thing and he answered, "It will be my happiness to serve you, my lord, both as a poet and as an architect. For I understand the making of arches and *Mihrabs*, of beautiful canopies for wells and the loftiness of towers from which the muezzin may cry. I know the making of bricks and paving of terraces and the laying in of marble and other stones. It will be my happiness if Allah so wills to see your land and write about it and to be your faithful and humble friend." And he looked into the agate eyes of Mansa Musa and saw him slowly and gently smile, his teeth gleaming white against the plum bloom of his skin. Yes, the African king had gold, but above all he was a man that a poet could love.

And so it was. The long march back began and went on

month after month, and suddenly a message came that one of Mansa Musa's generals had captured the city of Gao, the capital of Songhai. So he turned aside to receive the submission of the Songhai king and to take two of his sons as hostages. El Saheli the poet found a noble subject for a poem, but also he was bidden to make a new and better mosque for Gao. This he did and it was the first building in this part of the world to be made of burnt bricks.

So beautiful was this new mosque, so sky-piercing the minaret rising from it, that the poet-architect must next build a new mosque for Timbuktu. Nor did he build only mosques. He also built a terraced palace for Mansa Musa, putting into the building all the affection he felt for his noble and generous master. Nor did he lack for gold in his reward.

And long after Mansa Musa died people remembered his goodness and generosity and his power of ruling and administering what was by now a huge country, indeed an empire. And they remembered too that he was a black African from a scarcely known country, master of gold and best friend to a poet. And in the bad days centuries later when the Mandingoes were raided for slaves to be shipped to the American cotton fields, or later still when their country was taken by the French and the leader of the freedom fighters, Samori, was struggling against them, and today too when there is a new and independent Mali, men still remember Sundiata and his grandson Mansa Musa, the great kings.

The story of Sundiata is constantly told and retold by the griots of today, who still exercise their high profession in

Mali and are respected by all who care about history and the arts. It has been written down and translated in a fascinating book, Sundiata: An Epic of Old Mali, *by D. T. Niane, translated by G. D. Pickett (New York: Humanities Press). Much of the description of the trading cities comes from the Arab travelers who wrote down what they had seen, especially the admirable Ibn Battuta. His travels are published in the Broadway Travellers series.*

The empire of Mali went on successfully for many generations, but other kingdoms built up, especially two around Lake Chad, Kanem and Bornu. The next story is about the wars between Kanem and Bornu in the fifteenth century.

2 The Story of the Emir of the Faithful, Mai Idris Alooma of Bornu

The years went by. The caravans from the north still came and went, but sometimes it happened that they would hear the courts of the princes and rulers where they had intended to go were no longer safe for peaceable traders. Perhaps the towns where they had found hospitality were only heaps of ruin and ashes. For one kingdom after another took power. Sometimes it would be an able general revolting against tyranny or wasteful disorder. Sometimes a new sort of trade might be discovered. And just as in the old days the men with iron swords showed themselves stronger than the men with bronze swords, so the time came when the men with guns overcame the men with

29

swords and spears. The new empires spread north and east. The rulers were still Moslems, but the farmers and fishermen were pagans, at least until they came into the towns, where it was safer and courteous to go by the custom of the rulers.

Now, about two hundred years or a little more after the death of Mansa Musa, there was a certain Mai Ali of Bornu who married a princess of the Bulala, the riders on the red war horses. They were the rulers of Kanem at the far side of Lake Chad, toward the sun's rising. Now this princess, whose name was Aisa Kili N'girmaram, was dutiful and virtuous, and when her husband died she was able through the mercy of Allah to save the baby prince, his heir, from the wicked designs of his cousins, who would have murdered him so as to reign in his stead.

But they went the way of the wicked and Aisa Kili N'girmaram became Queen Mother and reigned wisely, building a high brick palace and a mosque fifteen miles from the city, lest her son should be corrupted by the sight and scent of luxury and the sound of profane music and the singing of dancing girls. But she saw to it that this son of hers, Mai Idris Alooma, had tutors of all kinds, so that he grew up wise and skillful in the arts of war and counsel. When he was a young man, he made the pilgrimage to Mecca and Medina and after that, having consulted with his captains and wise men, he went to war on Kanem. Now the rulers of Kanem were his mother's relations and all might have been friendly and peaceful but for their ambitions and the attempts which they made to claim and seize by violence three towns of Bornu and the fertile lands that went with them.

Now, when Mai Idris Alooma went out at the head of his army, there were men on foot with spears and bows and men in mail armor riding horses or camels. When the drums sounded, they marched and the dust rose thick into the heavens. Then, calling on the name of Allah, they charged and were victorious over the people of Kanem. This was a surprise attack and now there was coming and going and the army of Bornu halted. Mai Idris Alooma and his captains thought that the people of Kanem would surely fight back. But there came news that a man in the army had seen an egg fall out of the sky onto the head of one of the men of the Bulala and at that the whole army of Kanem had turned to flight.

There was more fighting and much depended on whether or not Mai Idris Alooma led his men to water for themselves and their beasts. For sometimes the men of Kanem would destroy the wells, filling them up with stones, and then Mai Idris Alooma had to command his men, half mad with thirst, to dig another well. But by the end of the march through Kanem and back to Bornu there were many captives as well as booty. Mai Idris Alooma gave orders that every man in his army who had so much as one prisoner should bring him or her in. Then when all were gathered together he divided the captives into free or slaves. The captives were all terrified, because in the days when the Bulala of Kanem had invaded Bornu, they made slaves of the free men and women whom they took prisoner and sold them to the slave traders from the north. How different was Mai Idris Alooma! "See," said his captains, and the Imams and the court poets who went with him, Moslems to a man, "see how God—exalted be He—

31

has endowed our Mai, the Emir of the Faithful, with high principles, goodness, and unselfishness!" The free prisoners were released without ransom, men and women alike, and only the slaves were divided up to be sold.

And the released prisoners showered blessings on him and many of them remembered that the Queen Mother had been a princess of the Bulala and they also called down upon her the blessings of Allah. But her greatest blessing was to see her son come back safe and sound and to know that he had dealt mercifully by his enemies and justly by his friends.

Soon after this, the people of Kanem again beat the drums and attacked Bornu. But the Emir of the Faithful would have none of this and marched so quickly that he surprised the army of Kanem, and although the horsemen escaped, he captured their camels and cattle and all their fine clothes and adornment and the women they had brought with them. So when Mai Idris Alooma came back he called together his people and spoke to them, saying that they must prepare for an expedition against Kanem before the date harvest, so that they should be able to do as much damage as possible and cut short the arrogance and violence of the rulers of Kanem.

So this was how it was done. The armies of Bornu marched, taking many prisoners, and all around the villages cutting down the half-ripe bunches of dates and eating the ripe ones or giving them to their beasts, and beating and abusing whatever of the men they could find. They marched quickly, although they stopped always for their prayers, kneeling on their prayer mats with their faces toward Mecca, to which some had already made the pilgrimage. But it was most necessary to find water for the army, although near the great lake at Chad there were marshes and green pasture.

By now they had taken so much booty that they could go back. Many of the rulers and captains of Kanem had fled, so there was much feasting and rejoicing. The riches were divided up and most of the prisoners were sold to the merchants, who were always looking for slaves to buy and drive to the north, in exchange for goods which were wanted in Bornu: various kinds of cloth and ornaments and spices, horses from Arabia, or, best of all, the new guns and gunpowder, although for many generations the people of Bornu had done well enough with spears and swords.

Yet Kanem was not yet conquered and another expedition went out. This time Mai Idris Alooma went more slowly, building great stockades around his camp, which made the progress of his army safer. But this time it was a harder war; the Bulala had strengthened themselves, beating the war drums day and night, and had armed and encouraged many of the tribes who lived in Kanem, whether Moslem or pagan. And they attacked with such vigor and courage that more than once they beat back the army of Bornu, looting their camp, rescuing the prisoners, and killing many of the captains and soldiers in Mai Idris Alooma's host. In one battle, indeed, the men of Bornu were swept off the hill which they were holding, leaving only the Emir of the Faithful himself, putting his trust in Allah and remaining firm on his gray charger, grasping with his hand his drawn sword, naked and sharp. And when the charger reared up to join in the retreat, Mai

33

Idris Alooma reined him back and made him face the enemy. And at that his men came back and again defeated the men of Kanem.

Yet things went none too well and on both sides the armies were weary of fighting and killing, and marching, and hunger and thirst. And there was less mercy shown and more slaughter and selling of prisoners. But then one of the leaders of the Bulala, Muhammad Ibn Abdullahi, who was close kin to the Queen Mother, Aisa Kili N'girmaram, the beloved of her son and her daughters-in-law, came to Mai Idris Alooma and promised to be his friend. There was joy then in the hearts of Mai Idris Alooma and of his mother and it seemed to the Emir of the Faithful that he had at last found a true brother. Muhammad Ibn Abdullahi swore on the Koran to be his friend and he brought over with him many of the captains of Kanem. At first they were afraid, but after a while they consulted together and in time a treaty was made by which Bornu took over some part of Kanem, but the rest was given to Muhammad Ibn Abdullahi to rule, for by now there was great affection between him and Mai Idris Alooma.

So all was well, and the army, instead of going out grimly in battle order, now wore their finest robes over polished and beautiful mail shirts, flashing in the sun as the spears were lifted and shaken, and their horses had glorious embroidered saddlecloths which floated in the wind as they charged, not now in battle, but for joy, and all passed in review before Mai Idris Alooma and those who had duly sworn peace with him. And after that even the Lord of Istanbul beyond the Middle Sea, the Sultan of Turkey, sent messages of friendship to his fellow sover-

eign, Mai Idris Alooma, far across the desert in the hot
south.

Yet these were not the last of the wars which were
fought by Mai Idris Alooma and the men of Bornu, for
there is always fighting when men become tired of peace
and the slow gathering of crops and increase of herds,
when they look for quick loot and power and violence and
the hard beat of the drum in the dawn and the hard knock
of the blood in the charge. But Allah gives victory where
he will. He loves mercy and wisdom, but injustice and oppression he punishes to the end of time.

*This account of the wars of Mai Idris Alooma comes from
a text that was found by the German explorer Barth and
sent to England, where later on it was translated. It is
called* The Kanem War of Mai Idris Alooma. *This was not
the last of his wars of conquest. But he also made the pilgrimage to Mecca and built a hotel for Bornu pilgrims
there. Yet in the end he was killed by a villager with an
iron hoe, desperately defending his family from the Bornu
slave raiders. From the time of Mai Idris on, for a couple
of centuries, Kanem-Bornu was an important central state.
But now we move farther south and back a little in time to
the state which spread inland from the mouth of the Congo
River.*

3 The Greatest Mani of Kongo

From far, from long ago, came the first kings of Kongo.
Ntinu Wene came with his companions, their war axes on
their shoulders, their deadly bows in their hands. It was he
who came to the mountain and challenged with drums and
trumpets, he who came to the fertile smiling lands on the
mountain top where the air was cool and the springs came
cold and pure from the rocks. All men acknowledged him
as conqueror and he took in marriage the daughter of the
chief priest, the Mani Kabunga, king of the spirits of the
earth, who thereafter brought the blessing of the great god
and showed him with what rites he could bring the other
gods and good earth spirits to his side. He showed him

37

also how to deal with the bad spirits, what sacrifices should be made, what things should be done or not done. These were the ancestors and through them he would be made royal. It was after all this that Wene, now enlarged by the spirits, became Mani Kongo, the King of Kongo.

Nor did his conquests cease; one clan or kingdom after another fell to his courage and strength. Forests and rivers were as nothing. The Mani Kongo charged through them like a bull elephant, fearing nothing. Lion and leopard to his enemies, to his friends he was like the palm tree, which gives food and drink, oil for light and health, and delicate fiber for finest weaving. After his time, the next king was chosen from among his sons, then from his son's sons, and so down the generations. The rulers of the provinces of Kongo, the anciently conquered kingdoms, who had all been appointed by the King, came together and chose the prince who seemed strongest. He, who was now above them all, in turn could choose whoever he wanted and raise him to be a Mani, a ruler, either in one of the provinces or in the capital itself, on the beautiful mountain top, ten miles around of cultivated land, full of busy villages. Here order must be kept. There must be justice and generosity. The royal guard must have weapons and fine plumed helmets and the best of food. Houses and decorations must be replaced and water channeled, all kinds of crafts must be carried on. Tribute must be paid and counted; it would come in as ivory, foodstuffs, palm products, and of course slaves, mostly prisoners of war.

Besides that, the Mani Kongo had an island in the sea and this island had long, sandy beaches. Women went down to the beaches, naked and singing, and lifted baskets of sand, which were also full of small, shining, pointed shells. The shells were sorted out into different kinds and some were used for necklaces, but most were used for coinage. If anyone went to a market, he must have a handful of shells to buy a basket of roots or fruit, a few cola beans, a spoon or a flute, a well-tanned hide, an elephant-hair necklace or bracelet, plumes of parrot or ostrich, or a piece of palm-fiber cloth. It was no use to have silver or gold; you must have the shells. A prosperous household would have a potful of shells like so many coins in a bank account. The fiber cloth was above all valuable and beautiful, supple and velvety, dyed and woven in patterns, or stamped with designs. For this was a peaceable capital; wars went on below in the forests; across rivers the war canoes charged and the bow strings zipped in the shadows, but not on the hilltop of Kongo.

So the years went by and there came a year when the villages along the shore sent word to Nzinga Kuwu, who was the Mani Kongo, the descendant of Wene, saying they had seen strange and huge whales far out at sea, and again in two or three years the same thing appeared. But this time the whales drew nearer to the shore at the mouth of the great Congo River and it appeared that they were huge canoes, for out of them came men and these men had pale red faces and much hair growing on them, and their bodies were mostly covered with cloth.

Word was sent to the King, but meanwhile his uncle, the Mani of the coast, welcomed them and was able in a while, and with all parties willingly eager, to speak with them. Now these ships had been sent by King João II of Portugal, under Diego Cao, partly to look for new lands from which Portugal could bring back by trade goods which might be easily got there but were scarce and valuable in Europe. They thought of gold, spices, ivory, strange animals, and slaves. In exchange they brought from Europe such things as linen or woolen cloth, beads and trinkets, mirrors and such. They also wished to gain souls for God and spoke much of their religion, of how those who had been baptized and who kept to certain rules would go to a heaven full of good things, while those who rejected this would be burned forever in hell. They showed the symbols of their faith, especially the Cross, which perhaps seemed to those of the Kongo who saw it like the tree which is also the backbone crossed by the path of living which is also the arms. The Portuguese expedition had with it priests, brave and devoted men; they named this the Year of Our Lord 1485.

All went well. The Portuguese spoke so much of the riches and wonders of their country that they found four young men from the noble families of Mpinda, the coastal town whose harbor sheltered their ships, who wished to go back with them. In their turn they left four missionaries who were sent inland to the court of King Nzinga Kuwu, the Mani Kongo. Two years later they came back. The young nobles of Mpinda were now dressed in Portuguese doublets and cloaks with swords and rings and handsome chains with holy medals; they spoke Portuguese and had all been baptized. They could not tell enough of the wonders of Portugal, the churches full of lights and statues, humming all the time with praises of God, the palaces with staircases so that one trod on the heads of those below and yet did not since there was a wall between, the glass in the windows, above all perhaps the horses on which men and women rode high and proud, or which pulled carts and carriages. They would have seen the great white oxen plowing and how even the poorest laborer wore some kind of clothing. These young men were now interpreters and receivers of gifts.

Meanwhile the Mani, uncle of the King, went to the forest and cut branches to make a green-leafed church, and altars were set up. Here he was baptized, leaving his old name of Mani Sogno for the new name of Manuel, while his baby son was named Antonio. Mass was sung and there was great happiness everywhere. The missionaries, who came down from the court of the King, spoke of the generosity and kindliness of the people and their willingness to hear the Gospel. They went back to Portugal with great praise of the land, fertile both in the material and in the spiritual sense, and praise also of the King's household and most of all of his mother and his son, Prince Mani Sundi, whose other name was Mvemba—"Mvemba of the bold eyes who looks steadily into the face of the lion." With them went an ambassador from the Mani Kongo and a number of young people to be educated in Portugal and to learn more of its wonders. And there were also great loads of ivory and palm fiber, and fabrics, as payment for their education.

The King also asked for craftsmen who could build him a palace such as had been described to him and would set up workshops for the making of all those charming and useful things which he had seen or heard of. So back from Lisbon in another four years came a shipload of artisans and missionaries and also of explorers charged with find-

41

ing the way to the fabled kingdom of Prester John. The missionaries made haste to build a church in the capital and then a school. Now they had banners and crucifixes, priestly robes and pictures of the saints. The Mani Kongo and all his family were baptized. The King himself took the name of the Portuguese king, becoming João I of Kongo. And his wife took the name of Leonor. Many of the nobility took the same step.

The ceremony had been hastened because there had been a revolt along the banks of the Congo; the war canoes were out. The King's son, Prince Mani Sundi—that is, the ruler of the Sundi Province—went in haste at the head of his soldiers with spear and bow, his arrows in a quiver of snake skin, his shield, his war ax, his belt of elephant hide, and his shining black necklace and armlets of elephant bristles from the tail of some great bull elephant. He himself led his soldiers in a shouting charge down on the rebels. Victory was theirs, and when the King himself came, all the rebels submitted. King and prince were carried back in triumph, umbrellas twirling over their heads, trumpets braying a conquest; behind them came trophies of ivory and cloth and many prisoners tied together. The Portuguese then made it known to the King and others that they would buy any quantity of slaves. Some were needed for the sugar plantations in São Tome, others to be sold still farther afield, for Portugal had already colonized a great part of South America and had sugar plantations there which must be worked. The South American Indians could be enslaved, but it was another thing to make them work; they died under the whips. The Africans survived and one might get many years' work out of them.

Meanwhile, Prince Mani Sundi offered himself for baptism, taking the name of Affonso. Many followed him. But his brother, Prince Mpanzdi, thought otherwise and remained in the old way of thinking. So did many others, including innocent wives who had been thrown out of their houses and sent back shamefully to their fathers because of the new Christian law which allowed only one wife. Thus there was increasing anger and hatred between the two parties, all the more because Prince Affonso seized and burned the masks and other symbols of the old gods and desecrated the ancient shrines of his people.

Yet Prince Affonso did this out of the belief that this new religion was truly noble and liberating and that he and his people could now claim Life Eternal through the Son of God. Affonso wanted to see his world made new with the new skills that the craftsmen from Europe had brought, the new trading prosperity which had come to the country, and the new idea of an approachable, loving, and merciful God. He and his friends were deeply enthusiastic. He himself carried stones for building the cathedral.

But the old King had somewhat lapsed, though it is said that he recognized great qualities in Affonso and wished to have him chosen by the electors, the rulers of the provinces, as the next king. However, when he died there was immediate war between the two brothers. It is said that Affonso had a heavenly vision and that he and his friends saw in the heavens above them a circle of five swords which, it seemed to them, were wielded on their behalf by the angels.

Prince Mpanzdi was either killed in battle or executed by Prince Affonso, who now was acknowledged as the

Mani Kongo. The priest of the earth spirits became the keeper of the holy water in the cathedral, and others turned with him to the King's religion. Above all, King Affonso would not have his own royalty depending on the old gods. He must be a Christian king and recognized as such. Yet somewhere in a dark place in dense forest was the House of the Great Images. Here by long tradition was kept the King's soul. Many of his friends, Christian though they were, begged him not to go there: let these things be forgotten! If he destroyed the House of the Great Images, the people of Kongo might turn against him. "If the King destroys his own royalty, what then? Will he still get victory over his enemies? Will he still make the crops grow and ripen the fruits?"

"I have faith," said King Affonso. "I trust in Jesus Christ that all will be well."

So he persuaded some of his friends to stand by him and he took Portuguese soldiers armed with arquebuses and together they went to the House of the Great Images. There were terrible noises, whistlings and gruntings and wailings; the Portuguese soldiers huddled together, but the King himself went ahead, unarmed except for his belief. He met the dance of the masked and terrible priests and dared to lay his hands on them; when he had torn off one mask and it was seen that under it there was only the withered face of an old man, all rushed forward and tore the masks and robes from those who had not escaped. The priests cursed him, saying that they would destroy his royal soul, but he was armed with his new faith. When the Portuguese soldiers put fire to the great House and the images, he comforted his friends, saying, "My soul is not destroyed. I see my Kongo as a kingdom of Christ. See what good things Christ has given to the white men. All shall be ours. We too shall have churches and schools. We shall learn all. We shall build tall houses and make guns. Our enemies will fear us and the borders of our kingdom shall be enlarged. And we need not fear death since at the end of our lives we shall fly up into eternal life. I, your King, tell you this."

So it was King Affonso convinced and strengthened his friends, who saw that although he was constantly going against the old beliefs, yet the kingdom prospered and the curses that had been thrown at him came to nothing. The capital became full of new things of which some were useful or beautiful, but all were desired by those whose eyes and hands reached out for them. Every year ships came and went between Kongo and Lisbon. Young men from noble houses went to schools in Portugal, among them King Affonso's own son, but they did not always learn useful things; sometimes they came back proud and lazy. King Affonso's army was armed and drilled by Portuguese captains and was the terror of the outlying tribes. A few muskets had been distributed, though nobody in Kongo understood how to make powder; the real power was left in the hands of the few men from Europe. The King of Portugal encouraged this traffic, thinking that a Christian kingdom in southern Africa would put bounds to the Moslem world, and thinking too that soon the Portuguese would find their way to the golden kingdom of Prester John, to which this might be the antechamber.

Yet those who went out from Portugal sometimes behaved badly; they cared only to get huge households of

45

slaves and they would not obey King Affonso's laws because they said they were white; masons and carpenters would no longer work with their hands but would only give orders. King Affonso complained of this in letters to his brother king, Manuel of Portugal, and asked him to send an emissary who would work with him and keep order among the Portuguese. And already he and a few of the wisest among his counselors were beginning to wonder whether it was altogether good to welcome these white people with such open hands.

King Manuel on this sent an ambassador, Simão da Mota, with a document in which his own wishes and those of his brother King Affonso were tied together, yet with some care so that Portugal should gain from it. It was suggested that Kongo should adopt Portuguese laws and also many European customs and titles. Simão was to act as counselor and would help King Affonso to make his court like that of Portugal. He must also expel any Portuguese who was living a bad or idle life, and indeed it was written in this document: "Our plans can only succeed if the men who carry them out are themselves virtuous."

More technical and military help would be given; more missionaries would be sent. But this must be paid for in slaves, in copper, or in ivory. The ambassador was instructed to study what other materials could be exported and how far north and east the great river could be navigated. And it was written that if the King of Kongo goes to war, "our own soldiers must never be taken to positions where they might be in danger, nor must war be allowed to turn to our own disadvantage." And again it was to be

46

hoped that Portuguese trading monopolies would be set up.

But King Affonso, although he accepted some part of this, knew that the leader of a country must never entirely abandon his own history and the ways of his ancestors. It would be foolish for the people of Kongo to become imitation Portuguese. Yes, let them be Christians, but they must keep their dignity as men and women. Their own laws could be softened by the Christian laws, but not utterly changed. If that happened, people would not know how to live rightly.

And at the same time the Portuguese, of whom there were more and more, began to quarrel about their trading rights. Not all the missionaries behaved well, and few of the traders did. But how could a Christian drink himself stupid, fall into a rage and beat his slaves, take bribes and think only of living in this world? How could one build a Christian state if such people set the example? More and more King Affonso thought of this and wrestled in prayer to try to find an answer.

And what was the trade which was carried on? It had started with ivory, timber, including the sandalwood out of which a scented powder could be made almost as good as that from India, parrots and other strange animals, and ostrich feathers. But by now it had become more and more a huge slave trade depending on King Affonso's wars. The first great caravan to be driven down to the coast, chained and whipped along, belonged half to a white trader and half to a priest. Some were shipped to São Tomé to work in the sugar plantations, others to Portugal, and from

47

there mostly on another still more dreadful voyage to the Portuguese colonies in South America.

Little more than ten years after he had come to the throne with such high hopes, King Affonso saw with deep trouble that this traffic was getting worse. "What shall we do?" he asked his counselors. "The only pay that a Portuguese will take is in slaves."

"We must do without them," said an older counselor at last, and muttered to himself. "Even the priests."

"And all our plans to become a Portugal in Africa?" said the King. "I see you all with fine cloaks and shoes. You live in stone houses with beds and curtains. You eat from silver. When you are ill, you take strong medicine from Europe. Your sons go to school. Few of our people know how to make these things, only a handful could be clerks or schoolmasters." Beside him knelt his own secretary, one of the first of the Kongolese to learn to read and write fluently. He noted what the King had said.

"We must go back to the ways of our fathers," said one,

48

but there were glances and headshakings. Nobody wanted to do that. Someone else said, "The guns?"

Another, who had only come to the capital a few days before, the Mani of a province, said, "Perhaps the King has not seen how far it has gone. In my own province the Portuguese come and set the small chiefs to fighting with one another so as to get prisoners. They buy from both sides. All the time it is harder to keep order. The King must throw out the Portuguese or they will destroy him."

For a time the King said nothing. It tore him to the heart to have had this vision of a kingdom of Christ, to have destroyed so much of the old order and tradition because of his faith. And now?

He had tried to curb the greed of the merchants and slave traders. He had tried to persuade them that this was no conduct for Christians and he had asked the best of the priests and teachers to do the same. But a few years later he was writing to his "brother" the King of Portugal: "There are traders everywhere in every corner of my country. They are bringing us to ruin. Not a day but some of my people are carried off in slavery: they do not even spare the royal family or the nobles."

It was useless. The profits on the slave trade were so huge that more and more of King Affonso's own subjects became involved in it. There were kidnappers everywhere. Rebellion was encouraged. Either way, it meant more slaves. Suddenly it became too much. The Portuguese had laughed at him, the slave trade went on. In deep anger the Mani Kongo decided to stop the slave trade and throw out all the whites except the missionaries. He knew that most of them had taken part in the evil thing, but he could not bear to face what their expulsion might mean. Mass must still be sung. God might call them to repentance.

But he failed. The slave trade had so corrupted his own subjects that they would not give it up. In the provinces nobody cared for the King's orders; even his messengers were no longer safe. His nobles were greedy, not now for the Life Eternal, but for the riches of Europe. They would seize and sell whole villages of people with only the smallest excuse. Crops would go untended, flocks would run wild because their owners had been sold as slaves. The best that King Affonso could do was to commission three inspectors, two of his own people and one Portuguese with a staff of clerks. Every purchase of a slave must be notified to this office and those who could prove they had been carried off were set free. Thus parents could now claim their children when they had been pounced on by raiders. Any trader who did not register a purchase would have all his slaves freed.

This, he explained in a letter to King Manuel, worked better for a time; at least the main trade went on at the capital and at Mpinda on the coast, where it was possible for the slaves to appeal for justice. But many of the Africans who brought in the gangs of slaves were themselves slaves, always under threat of being sold to the plantations or desperately trying to buy themselves out. The sugar-plantation owners of São Tomé had agents everywhere. Five or six thousand slaves were exported every year. The best that the King could do was to try and see that they came not from his own subjects but from the peoples beyond his borders, yet this meant that to protect his own people of Kongo he must be constantly going to war and making prisoners. He could not in any way get rid of the leeches who sucked the life blood of Africa.

But worse was to come. One year the Mani Kongo had sent as part of his enforced tribute to the cost of educating his young men in Portugal some silver rings which came from the King of Ndongo. This was one of the states to the south of Kongo which sent in tribute to Kongo but was in no sense under the government of the Mani Kongo or took orders from its stronger neighbor. That and rumors which came from the traders were talked over in Lisbon. The next thing that happened was that a group of German mining experts under the command of a Portuguese were sent to Kongo. But King Affonso refused to allow them to prospect; he saw that if mines were to be opened, these would be entirely for the profit of the Portuguese. They would demand more slaves to work them; his kingdom would be still further broken up. No, he said. No! And so said all his Council, although the Portuguese did their best with bribery and promises. But the Africans had seen enough by now. They knew.

Meanwhile the Portuguese did their best to stop trade between Kongo and other countries which might have broken their monopoly. French ships were stopped and seized. Nor yet, in spite of the letters which King Affonso wrote to King Manuel, did they send more or better priests. It seemed to the Mani Kongo that he must appeal directly to the Pope. Twice he sent ambassadors to the Vatican, but both were held in Lisbon and it was impossible for them to go to Europe except in Portuguese ships. It seemed to King Affonso that God had turned away. His prayers were unanswered. The only thing which was granted to him was that one of his sons who had been sent to Portugal for his education had become so enthusiastic and so well versed in theology that he was sent to Rome and as Dom Henrique consecrated as bishop. He came back to Kongo; he embraced once more his father, his mother, and his grandmother; he told them his plans for building schools and churches not only in the capital but in all the provinces. The King agreed; all went ahead. But there were not enough priests. Too many of the young men who had been sent to Portugal died with their education still not finished, struck down by the diseases of European towns: plague, typhus, smallpox; even the lesser diseases killed those who were unused to them. And Dom Henrique himself was ill. He died six years later, and although his funeral mass was celebrated with all possible pomp, and prayers said for him daily; although his parents knew him safe in Heaven, yet there was no one to fill his place. The Portuguese saw to it that there was no bishopric established in Kongo and that their Kongolese pupils did not advance so far in theology that they might be consecrated into the higher ranks. The King withdrew most of his scholars from Europe and stood firm against any opening of copper or silver mines. Angrily the Portuguese began to plot against him, hoping for a more pliable or bribable successor; but those from Lisbon tried one thing and those from São Tomé another. All that mattered to them were the profits.

How did it come that on the Easter Sunday of 1540 eight Portuguese broke into the church and fired on the King? He escaped and stopped his guards and people from massacring all the Portuguese. It was the last act of a real

Christian. Soon afterward he died, among his shattered dreams. He had kept his kingdom together. He had tried to accept the good things of Europe and not the bad; he had not succeeded, but he pointed the way for others.

This story has been pieced together from accounts which were written mostly by Portuguese. But we are lucky to have the actual letters of King Affonso. In another hundred years or so, the kingdom of Kongo was completely broken up by the slave trade. The Mani Kongo of that day allied himself with the Protestant Dutch, who were beginning to land along the coasts and could offer the European weapons against the Portuguese. He wrote in deep anger: "Instead of gold or silver or anything which serves as coinage elsewhere, here the coinage is people, who are not made of gold or silver or cloth but are living creatures. It is a shame on us and our forebears that in our simple ignorance we opened the door to so many ills, and above all we have permitted other people to pretend that we are not the overlords of Ndola and Matamba."

By that time Angola, to the south of Kongo, was in chaos. A fighting queen, Anna Nzinga, had allied herself with the sometimes cannibal Jaga, who had invaded from the interior: anything to get rid of the Portuguese! She offered protection to all escaped slaves and made them into an army, and tempted to her side the Africans whom the Portuguese had trained as soldiers. For years there was war; Queen Nzinga held out, with the support of all the oppressed. The Dutch came to her side when it suited them, but finally withdrew.

The breakdown of traditional law and order was com-

plete in both Kongo and Angola. Only the states and kings farther inland and out of reach of the slave traders survived rather better. We are gradually getting to know about them, partly through the patient digging out of records, often now by African historians.

Now we go to western Africa in the early eighteenth century. For now not only Portuguese but several other European nations, including the British, were beginning to trade along the coast. And the first country we shall come to is the kingdom of the Ashanti.

4 The Golden Stool of Ashanti

At that time Dankyera was chief among the Akan states that lie in the dense jungle of western Africa in the bend of the great rivers, between the haunted lakes and the toppling crags, country of elephant and antelope, of porcupine and leopard, fertile land when the jungle is cleared, and with streams where the sand is thick with gold dust. The King of Dankyera was called Ntim Gyakari. He had a clansman who was wise in all the mysteries of the gods, but the time came when he had to flee to a far-off place, where he became ever closer to the gods. His name was Okomfo Anokye and he became the greatest of priests and prophets. Above all, he came near to the supreme god of

the sky, Onyame, who is so great and so hard to understand or think about that no image is made of him, no sacrifice is made to him, who is beyond the thoughts and
doings of ordinary people, who instead must intercede
with his sons, the lesser gods.

Yet the supreme god, Onyame, had so far deigned to
interest himself in the affairs of mankind as to show favor
to the Ashanti people. For at this time Kumasi, the great
town of the Ashanti, was under the rule of Dankyera and
every year the King of Dankyera sent for his tribute, and
this was a brass pan filled with gold dust, and also the favorite wife and favorite son of every Ashanti chief. And so
great was their fear of the tyrant Ntim Gyakari that this
tribute was not refused.

There had been four kings of Ashanti, and the king who
ruled now, but always under Dankyera, was Osei Tutu.
He was a man of great beauty and royal appearance, and
as a lad he had been shield bearer to the King of Dankyera.
It was here that he met the wise Okomfo Anokye, who,
foretelling the future, helped him in all his doings. For the
sister's daughter of the King of Dankyera loved him, and
she it was whose son became heir to the throne.

When this was found out, Osei Tutu had to flee from
Dankyera; he went to another court, that of the King of
Akwamu, which was then also a strong kingdom, so that in
the end he knew much of what lay in the hearts of these
kings and their counselors. And Okomfo Anokye, ever
growing wiser in the affairs of prophecy and in the secrets
of the gods, watched this young man and was glad when
he was chosen from among the old King of Ashanti's

nephews—for the succession always lay with the sister's line—to be the new King.

Now, when he came to the throne, it was clear to Osei Tutu that there was scheming against him in the capital of Dankyera. Ntim Gyakari was jealous of him and wished to destroy him and his people. Secret messengers came and went through the forest paths, quietly, bringing news. It became clear to Osei Tutu that he must prepare for war. He spoke of this, guardedly, to his uncles and to the Queen Mother, Manu, who sat on his left hand, saying little but hearing all. She said to him: "There is the wise man, who has helped you before. He will know the mind of the gods on this."

And so thought Osei Tutu, and he sent word to Okomfo Anokye. "Come!" said the messenger, who was his mouth and who carried a golden staff whose head was a beast of the forest. "Come if the gods allow you."

Manu the Queen Mother knew he would come to the King, whom he loved and honored. "We will make ready for him," she said. So she sent out for the plants and animals which would be pleasing to the gods, and she and her women busied themselves with the necessary rites. Then the King sent out messengers, summoning his people to Kumasi, for he knew in his mind that Okomfo Anokye would in some way have prepared for him a great thing against his enemies.

So for many days thousands of men and women of the Ashanti nation came into Kumasi, all wearing beautiful beads and woven or printed cloths and ornaments of gold and copper and brass. Some wore the well-prepared skins of forest beasts; some wore kilts of palm-leaf fiber; many brought food and drink, driving in sheep and goats or carrying sacks of meal and roots, or great calabashes full of palm wine, and gave them to the King, who was able in this way to feed all that multitude. The lesser chiefs came with their queen mothers, the wise and gentle, who might be delicately marked with fine blue tattooing and so were perpetually veiled. The drums sounded all day and all night; dancers danced and the dust rose between the thick clay walls of the houses of Kumasi, splendidly decorated with raised patterns, and in the great open space where King Osei Tutu sat with his counselors and drummers and horn blowers, his executioners and his speakers, who when he wished to speak to the people made themselves his voices. They carried staves of gold and ivory, splendidly carved into animals and fruits and symbols. But the King Osei Tutu wore the most wonderful golden ornaments; on his fingers were many weighty rings, each made into some figure about which there was a story or saying. His wrists were weighed down by nobbled gold bracelets, so that he must support his hands on the shoulders of his servants. Around his head was a circlet of pure gold, and his sandals were heavy with golden lumps. His chest was bare so that all could see the strength of his breathing, and around his waist was the cloth woven in thin stripes of many colors which proclaimed him King, just as the cloths worn by the chiefs proclaimed their lineage. His mother, Manu, also wore gold, but her hair was gray and her breasts fallen, for she had borne many children. Yet without her word Osei Tutu would never have dared to come to any great decision.

Okomfo Anokye had spoken to them both, the King and the Queen Mother, in the dark of the night. He had spoken of a way of overcoming Dankyera, of making the Ashanti into a great nation, ruler of all the Akan states, trading with the caravans of the north, across Bornu and Kanem, and with the new white-faced strangers who were coming into the southern courts near the great ocean. Okomfo Anokye had made a dazzling prophecy of riches and powers. Manu had agreed first, then her son. They half knew what was to happen.

And now Okomfo Anokye was speaking to the Supreme Being, shouting, imploring. The blood of the sacrifice steamed up, the drums quickened and quickened. A black cloud seemed to gather; first a few saw it, then more, then all. It was blacker than a thundercloud, but thunder rumblings came from it. And there came a thick white dust, and then falling, slowly, slowly, turning like a seed, came the stool, with its base sending out three branches to support the shaped top. It glinted with gold, yet it was not entirely golden; below the gold it was carved wood. It fell more and more slowly and at last it came to rest upon Osei Tutu's knees.

The King was a brave man; had he not been bravest of the Ashanti, he would not have been the Chosen One. But now he shook a little and he could not put out one hand to touch the thing which had come from deep heaven. He had not foreseen that it would be like this. But Okomfo Anokye, himself also shaking with effort, had made ready elephant hides and cloths and laid them on the ground. He took the Golden Stool from the King, and set it on the cloths. Then he chose an albino with white skin, pale eyes, and reddish hair and sat him down on the stool. He touched this man on the head and it is said that his body disappeared utterly. His soul went into the Golden Stool, in great honor. And ever since that time, no albino has ever been put to death in Ashanti.

Then Okomfo Anokye spoke aloud to the King and to all the people, saying that now the Stool had been given a soul, and that now it had itself become the soul of the Ashanti nation and all their power was bound up with it. So the King and the Queen Mother, and each of the chiefs and his queen mother, gave hairs from their bodies and parings from the nails of their forefingers, so that their own souls should become one with this great soul. These were powdered and mixed with water and many other herbs and barks, and some was poured over the Stool and some was drunk. And it became clear that all the welfare of the people was in this Stool, and if it were ever to be captured or destroyed, so also would the Ashanti nation perish.

Nor could any mortal man, not even the King of Kumasi, sit on this Stool. In dire need the King must seat himself on his own royal stool, resting his arms on the Golden Stool. "And bells you must make," said Okomfo Anokye, the priest and prophet. "Two of gold and two of brass, and they must hang on the stool. Other things also will hang on it as time goes by. And it must have its own attendants and its own place, where it is greater than any king."

Now soon enough the Golden Stool showed its power. For Ntim Gyakari, the King of Dankyera, sent his envoy for the tribute. And the envoy came laughing. But no sooner did he come to the first of the chiefs, before ever he had made his way to the King at Kumasi, than this man, the Chief of Juaben, felt the new soul of Ashanti stirring within him, so that he rose up and struck down the envoy from Dankyera. Every other chief came and touched the blood of the envoy with his finger and swore to fight Dankyera and free the Ashanti nation. Then Osei Tutu set the talking drums to call up the armies and all came in good heart and, carrying the Golden Stool with them, totally defeated Dankyera. It is said that a hundred thousand men of the Dankyera were killed that day and the days that followed, and their country was so plundered and destoyed that it never again became a great power or a threat to Ashanti or the other kingdoms.

And further it is said that King Ntim Gyakari was found by the victorious army sitting bound with golden fetters and playing a game on a *worri* board with his favorite wife. Such was the power of the Golden Stool and the benevolence of the great god Onyame toward the Ashanti people that he did not even look up, so at once the two were beheaded and the golden fetters were fastened around the central support of the Golden Stool.

Other kings of Ashanti also made golden ornaments and put them onto the Stool, but today it is hidden and there are those who say it is all a story. But this is not the truth. For the courage and strength of a nation is a real thing, though it cannot be seen. And every Ashanti knows that somehow, in some way, the Golden Stool has gathered up and strengthened all that is best and finest out of the past and, if it is kept safe, will give it back to the men and women of today.

61

There are several versions of the story of the Golden Stool, but this is the usually accepted one. The stool of a West Coast chief is likely to have a soul of its own. It is a sacred symbol as well as a royal one. The stool at the top of page 55 is not, of course, the Golden Stool. But it is the stool of another West Coast kingdom.

Now we move east along the coast and into the Niger Delta, a century and a half after the first great rise of the Ashanti kingdom. By this time the slave trade was almost at an end. Most European countries, including Great Britain, had forbidden it. Queen Victoria and Prince Albert approved. It was just as easy to make a fortune out of the oil trade as out of slave trading.

You will find many strange and puzzling words in this story, but it is a twisted and tangled story. If you went to the same places today, people wouldn't really want, even if they could, to tell you about the Great Ju Ju of Aro Chukwu. All one can say is that Aro Chukwu was the center of religious power (as Delphi was for the ancient Greeks) and that there was an oracle there. The oracle, or its priests, demanded sacrifices and tribute; the god whom I call the High Power had to be feared or the tribute might not come. This was done through the King and through the local high priest at the main center (like Awanta at Ibani), who would see to it that all trading paid its tax. But what was the Great Ju Ju house like? We don't know, only that it was very frightening and very mysterious and that it smelled of death.

5 The Boy from the Bush

Ibani, which the whites called Bonny, was the greatest trading center of the Niger Delta, the richest of the city-states. Jubo Jubogha, who later was to be nicknamed Ja Ja, came to Ibani the hard way. He came with bruises on his body, feet and hands tied, hearing the chuckle of the dark, slithering water along the sides of the canoe that was taking him far from home. For Ja Ja had been a village boy deep in the Bush up the river from Ibani, bright and noisy, a leader in games and the hunting of small animals. Then one night the slave raiders came.

The boy was lucky that he was not shipped off to America or Brazil. The British had abolished their own slave trading and were instead encouraging the palm-oil trade —palm oil for greasing engines, for making the first cheap substitute for butter, and increasingly for making soap to use in industrial towns, which were getting dirtier every day. They had made treaties; the Royal Navy had taken and sunk pirate slavers. But, all the same, the trade was such a profitable one that there might be a dozen slavers hanging about the mouths of the oil rivers of the Niger Delta, and any of them would have given a good price for a likely twelve-year-old.

But he was lucky. Ja Ja was bought by one of the Bonny chiefs, though he was a wild boy, disobedient, too full of ideas. Punishment made no difference. Whip him and he came up smiling. His master could threaten him with ear clipping or branding, tell him he would be thrown to the crocodiles, but it was no use: he was a handsome boy and it would be a pity to spoil him. So his master gave him to Chief Madu, Head of the Anna Pepple House, greatest of the Ibo trading houses. This name was the English way of saying and writing the Ibo name Pelukele. When Madu died, his son Alali inherited the slaves, including young Ja Ja.

By now the boy must have been used to the great spread of the city of Ibani. Houses and houses: broad ways between them and then a tangle of walls, brown or painted plaster, the well-thatched roofs rising high in a cone behind. Sometimes he thought it was like the Bush, full of paths, some of which were luckier than others, places of gods or ghosts where it was best not to go at night but in the daytime bustle and laughing, a new song or a new saying running like fire. He went down to the Port, to the greenish-brown, dirty, heaving water pulled by the moon, full of ships, the great ships that sailed or steamed for Liverpool lying far out, and the small canoes of the traders jostling along the steps; a wonderful place for a boy, especially a boy who would run errands, could be trusted with money, would be guide to a stranger and always ready for a story. But above all, there was the great House of Chief Alali, his father; for the word "master" would not be used to a bright boy who increasingly was beginning to use his talents in the accepted way: by trade. Here, in the House of Anna Pepple were wide courtyards with shade trees and fruit trees, small vegetable gardens, the smoke and savory smell from cooking fires, children playing or learning, business going on. Here would be House worship and propitiation of the special House Gods.

The House of Anna Pepple was the Royal House, yet not in any way controlled by the King, who, because of his royal blood and because he was thought of as part of the High Power, could not engage in trade. Yet this High Power, the Great Ju Ju of Aro Chukwu, pride and terror of the Ibo people, could only speak through the King. Madu, the Head of the House, had been a slave himself, but had worked his way up through trade, until he was the richest man in the richest city of the Delta. He acted as Regent when the young King, William Dappa Pepple, was a boy. That had meant great power. When Madu died and was succeeded as Head of the House by his son Alali, the King began to work seriously against traders who had been slaves but had now got almost all the trade and money into their hands. It was intolerable that they should use their power to twist him and put their wishes to the Great Ju Ju!

So, when Ja Ja came to Ibani, the city-state was being pulled two ways. On one side was King William Dappa Pepple, his followers and advisers, and perhaps Awanta, the High Priest and direct representative of Aro Chukwu. On the other side were the great traders, the men who had been slaves. Some of them had been carried off from their villages as children; others had been born of slave mothers and free fathers. All had won their freedom by hard work and intelligence; they had educated themselves, even to reading and writing English; but still the free-born men liked to mock at them. But did that matter when they had Houses richly decorated with woven stuffs and bronze or carved wood? When they had wives and horses and slaves of their own, English and Indian cloth, not the worthless stuff that had been passed off in the old days but in first-class order and condition; when they had jugs and basins, scissors and mirrors, rum and brandy, guns and gunpowder, trading canoes and war canoes, all kinds of weapons, and in their warehouses valuable timber, camwood and others, as well as many puncheons of oil, and perhaps some ivory, all ready for shipping? When they dealt with the big traders from the ships or sometimes directly with the Liverpool merchant houses? Did it matter when they so much outnumbered the free-born men?

It was only that not one of them could himself be king, even though he might be made a chief. Not one, however powerful. Not Madu, not Alali. The people would only acknowledge the blood royal. This was the talk in the

Houses and in the markets or at the sacrifices. And the young Ja Ja got to know that a word from Aro Chukwu could bring a trade or lose it. The balance must be kept.

It was easy enough for a boy like Ja Ja to get together a few savings. Then he would get a paddle in one of the oil canoes and go trading up the river, buying cheap and selling dear. That was how it was if you were clever at it. And Alali, himself the son of a slave and someone who was often laughed at by the free-born, looked in a friendly and fatherly way at any young slave who seemed to be doing well, who might one day buy himself out and start trading on his own. Bonny had become rich by buying from the oil producers, the men who climbed the palm trees on the most propitious day laid down by the gods, gathered the oil nuts, cracked and pressed them, and sold the oil in the markets up the river and inland. The Bonny traders bargained and bought and carried back the oil, graded and bulked it, and sold it to the Liverpool and Glasgow men. The important part of this dealing was in a religious exchange which, in the pidgin English the traders used, was called to "chop Ju Ju." Here, Aro Chukwu and the High Power had their authority and their own part of the price. It was a balancing system. Alali let young Ja Ja go to the markets and look on and listen in to transactions, note how one put one's mark on a document, see how a good trader watched carefully the weight and quality of goods, not only those he bought, but those he sold. In the long run it paid to be honest, though there were times when one should be more honest than at others.

Chief Alali had the greatest of the Houses. Some of the Houses had only a few hundred people, some had thousands; they were like little cities within the great one. These were the security through which trade was carried on. A great House was a law to itself, but unless it was a reasonable and just law it would not survive. In most of the Houses the only free men were the immediate family; most would be men and women who had been bought or given to the chief, the head of the family, the father. Although there might be cruelty here and there, it was better and safer for the father of a House to rule by respect and affection than by force.

Ibani was a mixed city; there were men and women in it from all the southern tribes. There were more Ibos than others; yet the true inland Ibo, like the people of Ja Ja's native village, called the folk of Ibani "the people of the salt water." Once it had been a little village along a clean beach under a row of trees, but those days were long gone. Yet something from that time still went on. The fishermen had met at certain seasons and days for masked dancing and playing on special instruments. The women had been frightened or had pretended to be frightened, for in doing this the men had become one with the alarming ancestors. This still went on in the streets of the trading city and along the quay between the water and the warehouses. But now it might be the whites who were scared of the masks and the noises and the rushing feet.

For there were the whites. Some were good men, honest as Chief Alali, though addicted to a strange god. But others were rough and wicked; they thought nothing of putting a bullet or a cutlass through you and it was hard to bring them to justice. They were heavy drinkers and when drunk they would shout and swear that because you were black and they were white they could do what they liked. It was they who called Ibani by their own name, Bonny, and that was the name the traders used. These whites had many wonderful things, yes—but what they valued was the same that everyone valued: money.

Did Ja Ja ever see his native village again? Maybe not. Most likely the raiders had set a light to the thatch and later the walls had cumbled away in the rains and the Bush had walked in with creepers and thorns, with ferns and lilies, with palms and huge silk-cotton trees, with insects and snails, with butterflies and birds and small shy animals. And the people who were left made a new village somewhere else.

Perhaps Ja Ja never missed it or perhaps at the back of his mind there was always some kind of contrast between the innocence of the village and the commerce of the cities. As the years went by, he bought his freedom and became one of the respected traders of the House of Anna Pepple. All the traders of Ibani worked through the Houses, each House with its own head or heads. They made policy and regulated the flow of oil. But the King was increasingly against the traders. Above all he hated Chief Alali, the head of his old House. It was wrong that Alali was more powerful than he himself could ever be— he the true ruler! For it was he who went to Aro Chukwu and the seat of the god and was diligent in his support of the god's representative, Awanta, the High Priest of Ju Ju town, which was a little way from trading Bonny by road, but very far in thought. Here the bones of the enemies of

Bonny were so painted and arranged as to be forced into an after-death submission. This the King had seen himself; the submission was to him, the blood royal.

And which side were the whites on? Just one thing mattered to them: how to get treaties and agreements through so that their traders should be able to make as much money as possible, and as safely as possible. So Liverpool grew. The trade was worth half a million pounds, and an English pound was worth ten times as much a hundred years ago. A few were also interested in the spread of Christianity, but they too wanted safety in which to preach and teach.

Chief Alali wanted, above all, to keep Bonny independent. It was nothing to him whether trade was in slaves or palm oil, so long as it was their own trade, unhampered by treaties or special terms for one kind of white or another. The King played one against the other. The first to fall was Alali. King William Dappa Pepple himself entered into an agreement with the British and gunboats sailed and steamed about the great river and came increasingly into the port of Bonny.

But the second to fall was the King. He had warned the British that they were going too far. They had seized the High Priest of Bonny, the direct representative of the High Power, the hater and killer of the new Christians who threatened all the ancient ways of security. To treat the High Priest Awanta as a criminal, a common murderer, was sending shudders of fear and uncertainty throughout Bonny. All was falling to pieces.

But the British knew that when this falling to pieces happened, it was possible for them to step in, and for

themselves to become the rulers. And where they stepped good things would follow, not only for Liverpool and Glasgow but for Africa. Not only palm oil but cotton might and should be grown, cotton for Lancashire, money for Africans who would spend it on British goods. But those kings and chiefs who tried to restrain trade must be cut down in size or abolished.

It ended with the exile of King William Dappa Pepple along with his son George. Whether or not he left willingly is something else again. Whether the people of Bonny felt that when their King left them, part of their luck, their god, also left them is not plain. But the blood royal must still hold the Stool of Bonny. The people chose young King Dappo. He was blood royal, but in all things he took the advice of Chief Alali, who came back when King William was exiled. And so it came about that the House of Anna Pepple and all those trading within it became greater yet. And among them was the young trader

Ja Ja, now a free man with a household and slaves of his own, with his own trading canoes and a share of the Anna Pepple warehouses on the port.

When King Dappo died, there was a flare-up between Chief Alali's party and the party of the kings. It ended with a complete victory of the trading Houses and the ex-slaves, led by Alali. It must have seemed to some, at least to those who had been slaves, that now their time had come. They, not the free-born men, were the bravest, the cleverest, and above all the richest. Ja Ja, who had lately been accepted as a chief, would have felt like this, and he would have felt deeply grateful to his father, Chief Alali, who had wiped out the stain of slavery from all his House. When Alali died, Ja Ja must have wept, and made the necessary sacrifices and dances as truly as any son in the flesh.

Who would be the new head of the Anna Pepple House? There were debts to be paid. A great trader could pay them out of his profit, but many were afraid to take them on. But after a while, and after all the others had come together to press him to accept the headship, Ja Ja said yes and pledged himself to the traditions and customs of the House. This, in his eyes at least, meant acceptance and support of the national religion; he went through the rites and himself became a priest.

By that time the old King William had been brought back from exile, and with him his son, soon to be his successor—George, who did not care for life in Bonny, who longed for the London of Bond Street and Gilbert and Sullivan, but also for the stability and doctrines of the Church of England. The Crown Prince did not feel the pulse of the politics of his city-state, and he hated the shadow and smell of Ju Ju town and the priests, although for most of the people of Bonny, when they thought of their royal blood, they also thought of their god. The old King and his son had come back to debts and miseries: although the British provided a little steamer, the royal oil trade was small compared with that of its rivals. And behind them, giving support and money for their sometimes expensive needs, was another ex-slave, Oko Jumbo, who had broken with Alali and Ja Ja.

Now, Oko Jumbo was head of the other great House, which was called by the whites Manilla Pepple. He was a Christian. He himself learned to read and write and sent children to the Christian school started by the Yoruba Bishop, Samuel Ajayi Crowther. He was convinced that this was the modern thing and would mean that Bonny would be accepted on terms of equality by those other Christians—the British. Seeing that both Oko Jumbo and the Crown Prince were Christians, many followed them. When the old King died and the new King George succeeded him, all seemed set for the success of the missions. How much easier it would be for the British consuls, the traders, and Her Majesty's Navy to deal with a Christianized, Europeanized state in which everyone would make a new start to a new history, on acceptable and profitable lines, where the Union Jack would be duly honored, and other European nations would be obliged to go elsewhere if they wanted to trade!

But Ja Ja had seen the face behind the mask. He knew that any real independence for Bonny, and indeed for any state along the Delta coast, could lie only in keeping the whites at arm's length, trading honestly but never submitting, never allowing themselves to become in any way obedient or grateful to the Europeans and their god. He could see what had happened elsewhere along the coast. People had taken the European ideas and discarded their own order and their own traditions. Everything went into chaos. Then the European judges and officials came and took power. Was this to happen in Bonny?

He was preparing. For one thing, he found plenty of intelligent young men belonging to the House, slaves or only lately free. He bought canoes for them, helped them to trade, and guaranteed them to the Europeans. How the other slaves must have talked! How they must have wanted to be Ja Ja's men—Ja Ja, the rewarder of merit; Ja Ja, who laughed at the boasts of the free men! He himself prospered. He paid off the debts of his father, Alali, and gathered guns, cannon, and above all loyalty and popularity. Also he became Chief Priest to the Ju Ju House. When he was ill, he refused to listen to the missionary who would have liked to cure and convert him at the same time. He sacrificed to his own gods and recovered.

Oko Jumbo and the House of Manilla Pepple became increasingly alarmed. Ja Ja must at all costs be stopped. A state of tension built up; a fire broke out and destroyed part of Bonny, including many of Ja Ja's warehouses. Now might be the time. War was declared. Ja Ja sent his women and children to the Ju Ju town, where they were all slaughtered by the men of Manilla Pepple. But they, in turn, sent their women and children to the strongly guarded mission house, where they were safe. This showed Ja Ja at his most intelligent. He pretended to have lost; he appealed to Consul Livingstone; he placed himself under the protection of the Queen of England. Oko Jumbo was willing to accept a truce; he did not even want to crush Ja Ja completely. There was talk of a huge fine.

But meanwhile Ja Ja had slipped away with his canoes and guns and cannon eastward into the Andoni country, and here he had established himself. Perhaps he had intended this all along. It was a wonderful position, where the brown, sluggish, navigable creeks came down from the palm-oil country and met at a great market. Here he made agreements with all the principal chiefs; he told them what kind of state he intended to set up, and they chose him as King.

Ja Ja, the Bush boy, the slave, could never by any possibility become King of Bonny. Instead, he was now King of Opobo, and also its High Priest. He called his state Opobo after the greatest king of Bonny; he had, so to speak, taken the spirit of Bonny and enlarged it. But Bonny itself was cut off from its oil market, and this would be the end of it unless somehow the trade at Opobo could be stopped. But there was this difficulty for the rulers of Bonny; Ja Ja had already got two European traders onto his side. Others followed, and so did some of the chiefs of Bonny, those who were not involved with Oko Jumbo and the House of Manilla Pepple.

King George had taken the side of Oko Jumbo and the Christians; he was horrified by what Ja Ja had done, not merely because it was ruining Bonny but because it was a

win for the heathen. He knew, too, that those who protected missionaries had strong advocates, not only in the
courts of heaven but in the courts of England. Besides, he
knew—as Ja Ja did not know—that in the end, England
was far stronger than Bonny or Opobo, or indeed the
whole of the west-coast states put together. Britain might
be slow to move, but in the end there were the great ships
and cannon, which could outshoot anything that the Africans had. King George was also aware that he had true
friends in England who sympathized with him, and in
high places. He appealed to them over the head of Consul
Livingstone, and this sometimes made for difficulties.

However, for the time Ja Ja had won. He was Opobo.
He was indeed willing and anxious to trade, but on his
own terms, which meant that he would take from Europe
only what he could understand: first, money. Then arms,
including three Galting guns. Then, oddly enough, education. Emma Ja Ja, the schoolmistress, with sixty boys and
girls diligently learning the three R's plus English, had
once been a Miss White, daughter of slave parents in Ken-
tucky, who in her middle age emigrated to Africa and became Ja Ja's secretary as well as schoolteacher.

Ja Ja received English visitors so long as they did not try
to convert him or otherwise act as moral or social superi-
ors. All were impressed with his intelligence, and with his
charm when he chose to exert it. Their places at state ban-
quets were set with knives and forks, and their glasses
filled with dry champagne. The knives and forks were im-
ported, but the plates were African pottery, the work of
skilled women potters. Ja Ja himself never touched alco-

hol, saying that no African ruler should demean himself with drunkenness, though he allowed his chiefs to drink the local palm wine. He would, on occasion, himself wear European clothes, but preferred to wear cloth elaborately woven in brilliant colors and coral glinting around his neck. This was the robe of royalty. Above all, he kept absolute order, though perhaps by absolute rule.

War went on with Bonny, and the white traders sold guns, shot, and powder to both sides. Some had made arrangements with Ja Ja; others had warehouses and interests in Bonny. The war canoes fought and the crocodiles were well fed. The British Foreign Office was not anxious to interfere in a war they could not understand. Ja Ja was one more name. Some of them perhaps realized that when English traders began to go into the interior and trade directly with the growers of palms and pickers of oil nuts, the Africans, who had built up this trade themselves, would react. They were nobody's fools. Here and there some African could be made drunk or bribed into letting a European boat through into the market. But Ja Ja was adamant. All trade went through him. It was death to any trader who thought otherwise. At the end of his war with Bonny, and in spite of King George's sad attempt to show that English law was on his side, Ja Ja was formally recognized by the British as King.

Meanwhile, the missionaries were pressing him to allow them to open stations at Opobo. Ja Ja knew that this would mean the breakup of his order. Instead of being part of a community bound together in ritual and sacrifice to the High Power and the gods of control, whose priest he was, the Christian converts would think only of their own individual souls, their individual sins and repentances. Converts would begin to burn temples and to kill the great lizards that were sacred to the god and brought luck with them, the lizards whom he thought of as his children. He knew that after the missions there would be trading stations, and the whites would be one step nearer to the inland markets. He knew also that if he allowed missionaries he would be in favor with the British government as King George was. So he temporized, affecting to be persuaded, and finding his greatest opponent was Bishop Crowther, who, like himself, had once been a slave but had found another way out.

Over another problem he was much more definite. There were by now many educated Africans who had been to school—some even to England itself—and who, although they were not chiefs or members of Houses, wanted to trade. Many were not Ibos; they came from as far along the coast as Sierra Leone. Their language and customs were not his, but they were fellow Africans; it was enough. The English traders tried hard to keep them out and persuaded the Liverpool shipping companies to refuse their oil or their shipments from England. King Ja Ja put his foot down. Either Africans were to be on a complete trading equality with the whites or there was to be no more trade for anyone. He won. And he gave the African traders a monopoly in the sale of goods from Lagos, which was already a manufacturing town.

Yet King Ja Ja was up against something so big that he could not apprehend it, any more than an individual white trader could have done. He was facing the force of imperialism, of a European world suddenly made rich by machines and the inventions that went with them, immensely powerful and unable to escape from this power, which was driving its new riches outward. Before Africa could stand against this, it too must generate a force stronger than any one kingdom.

Nobody saw it like this. Not the African Association—the Glasgow and Liverpool firms who complained to the Foreign Office that their agent in the oil rivers was being obstructed from trading by Ja Ja of Opobo. They only saw the interference with their profits. Not the Royal Niger Company, trading farther along the coast but aware of what was happening and hoping in time, to get all the companies under their net of monopoly. Not Consul Harry Johnston, whose appointment was a threat which Ja Ja at first did not see. Not Bishop Crowther, intent only on the work of God. Not Oko Jumbo, trying to get back to his old position of power and riches. Not King George Pepple, wishing he could revisit his London friends, who would see matters just as he himself saw them. Not the captains and admirals of the British Navy. Who sees far beyond the immediate action that must be taken? Only the greatest, and with them only by moments.

And Jubo Jubogha, the Bush boy, how far did he see? He had left the city of Bonny, where he had been sold as a slave, punished as a slave, but had been given and had taken his chance. Perhaps he hated the world of Bonny, the lies and bargaining, the half acceptance of the things of Europe. He still had to lie and bargain with the outsiders, but not with Opobo, where he, Ja Ja, was keeper of order and certainty, the spirit of old Ibani—what Bonny had been before its corruption. "I, Ja Ja, am Africa."

But the African Association of Glasgow and Liverpool firms, backed by the British consuls, and especially by Consul Harry Johnston, always anxious to add another bright jewel to the Imperial crown, was inevitably the winner in the end. The Royal Navy was brought in, some-what reluctantly. The Foreign Office supported their consul against Ja Ja, though Lord Salisbury wished to hear Ja Ja's deputation, which was on its way to England. Ja Ja was trapped, or persuaded into a meeting, with the guns of the Navy waiting to bombard Opobo; he was deposed and deported to the West Indies in 1887. Salisbury commented: "We need not discuss the principles developed in this despatch. They amount to this: if a merchant differs from a native chief as to their respective rights, the native chief is to be deported."

Now we go back in time and a long way in space, across hot, tangled forests and grassy plains, over great rivers, five hundred miles and more, into southern Africa, the country of the Nguni, which is now Natal. But when young Chief Senzangakona went dancing with the maidens and one of them loved him too well, settlers from Britain had only just landed. They were holding precariously to a few places along the coast, south of the Portuguese and north of the Dutch, and wondering what the interior of the land could be like. It was the year 1786.

Before coming to these southern African stories, you may like a note on the African plurals, which I am bound to use sometimes. Among the Nguni people, Ama is the general term: Amazulu means Zulu people; Amandebele, the Ndebele people. But in the Sotho group of languages, which includes both the Sotho and Tswana people, the plural is Ba. I write either of the Kgatla people or the Bakgatla, while Kgamanyane was—and I myself am—a Mokgatla. The language prefix is se—Sesothos, Setswana.

6 Shaka of the Amazulu

The little boy had been given a shameful nickname. He should never have been born. His father, the young Zulu chief, Senzangakona, would not acknowledge him. All the other children teased him and he flared back at them, hating them. The children were all sent out together to herd the calves and goats when they had been driven out from the kraal, to see that they went far enough to gaze but not so far that the leopards or lions could pounce on them. The children went naked in the hot sun among the grass and flowers, or perhaps wore a few beads. They pulled switches off the bushes to herd the goats, but often enough

83

the switch would come down on little Shaka, the Belly Beetle, Shaka the fatherless.

Being one of the Amazulu—and a member of the Nguni people—Shaka did not cry, not even when they made him eat scalding-hot porridge or threw insults at him which were more painful still. He knew that one day he would beat them all. But whenever things became very bad for him, he would go to his mother, Nandi, for comfort and encouragement. In her arms, at the back of the dark hut, he could cry his eyes out. She had been taken as a junior wife for a short time but later cast off by his father and was living with her own people. Yet sometimes his father's Chief Wife, Mkabi, who had always befriended Nandi, came to visit them, and she too gave love and encouragement to the little boy and great praise when he killed a deadly snake which had attacked the best bull of the tribe.

Yet, as he grew up, tall and strong, quick to anger, but more and more able to best his attackers, his father thought that after all he might acknowledge him. But Shaka, although, he had gone through the rites that among the Nguni people made him a man with others of his age group, would not take the growing-up gift, the apron of softly tanned hide which his father would have given him. Because he loved his mother so much, he was bound to be angry with his father, and still more deeply angry with all those who had mocked and ill-treated him and his mother during the hard years of his childhood.

Soon after this there was a famine. Only too often famine came in southern Africa if the rains failed. Then the crops withered and there was no grass to feed the cattle and goats, no pools of water for them to drink at. People

84

moved as they could, and so Nandi and the young Shaka, hungry and footsore, moved to another clan of the Nguni. After a while they settled down happily, and Shaka's foster-father, Mbiya was kinder to him than ever his real father had been or was likely to be. Here Shaka got on well with the other herdboys and learned with them, as all young Zulus learned, to revere and obey his seniors, growing always toward manhood, as a girl in the same way grew toward womanhood. As a boy became older, so he took on more responsibility for others, and this meant learning how to use weapons, but also how to control his temper, so that these were not used wrongly. And at the same time the growing boy, giving obedience and respect to those older than himself, above all to his father—or, for Shaka, his foster-father—and his village headman, saw young boys give him respect and obedience. He must be generous to them, sharing food with the little ones and helping them, showing them how to do their tasks so that each had a place in the kraal and all were happy together.

The boys played weapon games that fitted them both for war and for hunting; for the grazing grounds were full of dangerous wild beasts. Shaka had been given a small shield and a few throwing spears—assegais. He practiced with them, and also in the mock fights, which had strict rules, so that no boy was allowed to damage another. Shaka's group was always the best and Shaka himself became the leader, the best dancer, the teller of jokes and singer of old stories and new; many of the older men must have watched the doings of this tall, beautiful young man and prophesied great things of him, all the more when he killed a leopard singlehanded, a deed which won him great praise and the gift of a cow from the headman. How he must have longed for a time when he too could be generous, a giver of cattle, above all to those who had helped him and his mother!

At this time Dingiswayo was chief of the Mtetwa tribe, one of the most powerful among the Nguni. He was a brave and capable man who at one time had conspired against his father and had to flee. On his travels he had learned to observe much, and one of the things he had seen was the white men who had come in ships and had made themselves houses on the African coast. They had horses to ride, the strangest of beasts, but still more important were the noisemakers, the guns that killed from far off. By all means, thought Dingiswayo, we must trade with them, but what if many come? What if they try to steal our cattle? But he did not think, what if they steal our land? Because, in his mind, he could not consider land as belonging to any one person or clan but as something as free for all as the air he breathed. Yes, cattle belong to people and crops belong, but not the land which grew the grass or the sorghum and millet grain that the women hoed and harvested. Yet, for the time being, these strange, red-faced, hairy men who wrapped themselves in cloth, perhaps because they were so ugly, were no threat and the things they brought in were useful.

But Dingiswayo also saw that it was better to have one Nguni nation. If the threat ever did come, all must stand together, so he set out to conquer other tribes and clans or to persuade them to acknowledge him as overlord, and to do this he called up the age groups in regiments, or *impis*, of young men. Now Shaka was a soldier of the Izi-cwe

86

impi, with a great oval shield of oxhide that could cover almost all of his body, with war assegais and sandals, a dashing kilt of fur strips and a decoration of oxtails and feather plumes. Wearing this, he was the best of dancers, leading his friends, a storyteller with a hundred riddles and double meanings on the tip of his tongue.

The Izi-cwe *impi* practiced for war, and during this Shaka tried two new things. One was to throw off his heavy oxhide sandals and the other was to keep back one assegai to use at close quarters as a stabbing spear. And this he thought would be better still if it could have a heavier blade and shorter haft. This thought kept on coming back into his mind, even while he was making love to his sister's friend, the beautiful, wise girl Pampata, the dark pair of them lying and whispering together on his great oxhide shield.

And so it was that he went to the best craftsman of the blacksmith clan and told him of his need. The smith saw that it was no common man who asked this thing of him, even though he proclaimed himself only a poor soldier of the Izi-cwe. So he did all things well, strengthening both himself and Shaka with powerful medicines, while he smelted out the iron for the new blade, forging and tempering it, surrounding it all night with magic, at last sharpening and hafting it, with Shaka watching, himself shaken by the magic but intent on the birth of the new weapon, which later, when it had killed, was called Ixwa.

And now the Izi-cwe, after they had been doctored for war through the ritual killing of a great black bull, were sent out against the Butelezi clan, who met them in a narrow valley. The men who were to be Shaka's best friends,

Ngoboka and his comrade Mgobozi, saw that Shaka went barefoot and that above all he had this wonderful stabbing spear. So did others, and this was the beginning of the conviction that Shaka knew more than any other warrior and that those who followed him, doing as he did, would go on to certain victory. The bravest and most famous of the Butelezi warriors stepped forward, offering to fight Dingiswayo's champion in single combat, as the custom was. Shaka leaped from his place, advancing with the terrible new weapon. His shield turned the thrown spears of the Butelezi champion, and a moment later the stabbing spear, Ixwa, went through him from one side to the other while Shaka shouted "Ngadla!"—I have eaten.

Then with the dead champion bleeding into the dust, Shaka rushed at the Butelezi and might have been overwhelmed but that Ngoboka and Mgobozi and then the whole of the Izi-cwe *impi* tore after him, shouting, like a stone thrown into honeycomb, and broke the Butelezi front. After this, when the Butelezi chief had submitted, Dingiswayo sent for Shaka and questioned him, hearing about and handling the stabbing spear. He called up the regiment and from them Shaka and Ngoboka and Mgobozi; all were praised and given cattle and the Izi-cwe shouted for pleasure and pride.

After this, one clan after another submitted to Dingiswayo. Shaka was always in the lead; where he went, victory followed. He slew the terrible mad giant, the smoker of *dagga*—hemp—who had put fear into the whole countryside. This brought him praise and cattle. He drove the cattle back to the kraal of Mbiya, his foster-father. Now he was able to get beautiful beads and bangles for his mother, for his sister Nomkoba, and above all for Pampata, who had given the beads which are a girl's pride and pleasure, in exchange for charms to keep her hero safe.

But before that he had been with Dingiswayo, who spoke to him now as a favorite son, saying that he would see to it that he became the next chief of the Zulus and had put him in command of the whole regiment, the most praised of the *impis,* bidding him to be careful, for he was too good to lose. Dingiswayo also told Shaka of the white men and what they did. They were very powerful and very greedy. They could not have enough. Even if there was good rain and good grass, they would chase away the cattle of other people from grazing near their own kraals. And it seemed that there were more and more of them every year coming over the great water in houses with wings and settling like flies on a carcass. Some called themselves Dutch and some English. But the worst was, they did not stay in the one place; they moved out and if ordinary people were in the way they would kill them with the iron sticks they called guns.

"They will never come here, my Father," said young Shaka, and in the movement of anger he made the muscles ripple on his splendid shoulders and chest.

"Who knows, my son?" said Dingiswayo. "It is like a river coming down after the rain; you think it will be nothing, but in a moment you are under the water."

"They would not dare!" said Shaka, and he smiled, thinking of the new spears.

"You have not seen what they can do," said Dingiswayo,

89

"from far off. And yet—if we could all be together, all of the Nguni, if we could trust one another! Only then could we beat them back."

"If we were one nation, my Father," murmured Shaka. "It is so. It is so."

Now Shaka began seriously to train his regiment in the new tactics he had thought out, a central attack with the sides splitting off to encircle the enemy—breast and horns, as it was called. In peaceful times there was also much dancing, but peace could not last long when Dingiswayo had enemies such as Zwide, chief of the great Ndwandwe tribe to the northeast. He was the son of a witch queen, Ntombazi, the woman who, they said, rode hyenas through the night, whose evil-smelling hut was full of the skulls of her own and her son's enemies. At the council of war, Shaka spoke of the need for all to be armed with a stabbing spear and demanded the complete destruction of Zwide. But the older commanders hated the thought of the stabbing spear and the bare feet, and Dingiswayo hated to destroy any of his fellow Nguni.

In a great battle Zwide and his Ndwandwe were totally defeated, mostly by the use of the new tactics and by the immense courage and dash of Shaka, who was now called Si-gi-di, Finisher-off. This became the Zulu war cry. Zwide was taken prisoner. A vast amount of cattle was taken, and Dingiswayo decided to give a royal-sized herd to Shaka, his young general. But Shaka refused to take more than a few, saying that all his soldiers had done well and most of the cattle should go to them. And he begged Dingiswayo to kill not only Zwide but also the old witch queen, Ntombazi. "If you do not kill them, my Father Dingiswayo," he said, "one day they will kill you and the old witch will hang your head in their hut."

But Dingiswayo felt that he could best bring the whole Nguni nation together without too much bloodshed and misery. He fined Zwide many oxen, said that now they must be friends, and Zwide agreed, but in his heart he hated Dingiswayo, who had put him to shame, and when he went home his witch mother comforted him, saying the time would come when Dingiswayo would lose his head. Then Zwide would be chief of all the Nguni!

Shaka was at home with his stepfather, Mbiya, his mother Nandi, and especially his love, Pampata. But he had made up his mind never to marry, never to father a son, never to repeat the story of his father Senzangakona and himself. But he told his mother that now that he was Dingiswayo's general and favorite, everything would be made up to her, all those who had befriended her would be rewarded and her enemies punished, yes, punished! And his anger flared again and now he knew he could quench it in blood.

Shaka was made commander of all Dingiswayo's armies, and a member of his inner council. He remembered his friends and helped to install Ngoboka chief of the Sokulu clan, himself laying the leopard skin, the symbol of chief-tainship, on Ngoboka's shoulders. Senzangakona, who was half attracted to his son, Shaka, and half in fear of him, had died, leaving the chieftaincy to another son, but the boy was killed and Shaka became the King of the Zulu people. He was shown to them, wearing a wonderful headdress of scarlet loury feathers, and high in front, one blue quivering feather of the wild crane. All accepted him, some in fear but most in joy.

Now he began to remake the armies, above all arming them with heavy spears. And now, too, he began his revenge on all those who had slighted or hurt his mother and teased or hurt him as a little child. They were mostly his own relations, the royal blood, descendants of the first Zulu, the sky hero. Some had been big boys when he was a child, the tormentors from whom he and his mother had clung together, hungry and miserable, their tears mixing in the back of the hut. One small act of kindness in those days saved the men who were dragged in to be judged by the Great Elephant, Shaka the wholly-powerful, or who walked proudly, knowing themselves doomed. The easiest death for any of them was by the spear or by the club, but the worst of them were given the worst kind of death, though it seems that Shaka himself hated the sight and sound of it; he was a man torn within himself. Only Pampata could always soothe and help him with wise and gentle counsel; she knew, too, what was said behind his back and could prepare him. For an African leader must never go too far from the mind of his people.

All had to learn the hard way. His soldiers must throw off their sandals, so as to be the fastest runners in the world. He had their parade ground strewn with the terrible three-pronged seeds whose thorns would go through a leather-shoe sole; here they must dance, chanting their war songs, until the thorns were trampled out of sight. Shaka himself led them, but his feet were hardened by barefoot years; he watched. Whoever flinched was clubbed to death.

Yet with all this, not only did he keep the loyalty of his own comrades, Ngoboka and Mgobozi, but other brave and ambitious soldiers flocked into his service; there was constant fighting and extending of Dingiswayo's rule, but Shaka still considered Dingiswayo his father and chief and always honored him. Meanwhile, he began to breed his cattle for pure colors or the special markings and fleckings which seemed most beautiful to men whose lives were spent so much in thinking about cattle. His mother, his sister Nomkoba, and his half sisters—especially those who had been kind to him—were put in charge of the many girls who had been taken in war or given to him.

When his old comrade, Mgobozi, asked permission to wear the headring, the sign of manhood, Shaka agreed, saying to all those around him, "Many a day Mgobozi was my shield in battle. But for him, I would be dead. Now comes his reward." And in a matter of days Mgobozi's new kraal was built, with many huts and a central stockade for the cattle. "And now that you are a full man, you will marry?" said Shaka, smiling.

"Yes, Great Elephant," said Mgobozi.

"And how many wives shall it be for this great kraal you have?"

"I have spoken to one or two and it seems that they see me with soft eyes, but their fathers think only of cattle."

"So I must find the cattle, Mgobozi, and melt the hearts of one or two fathers. Or is it, when you say one or two, you mean twenty?"

And indeed twenty it was, and it is said that Mgobozi, the great fighter, was in more trouble than he had ever been in his life, for he had promised each of the maidens that she would be the Great Wife, so there was plenty of laughter and perhaps some anger during the wedding festivities while the songs were sung and the presents of food and drink, of beads and plumes, of mats and cooking pots and snuff spoons, of knives and baskets and carved trinkets, were passed between the singing, laughing, dancing groups. And always Shaka was there as the chief guest, queller of disturbances, and acting father to Mgobozi, to whom he said, "Now you are in the cooking pot and twenty brides are holding down the lid!"

But he himself still thought of war and spoke of it to Dingiswayo, who always counseled moderation, shaking his head over some of Shaka's killings. When he went home and found his foster-father, Mbiya, dying, it is said that Mbiya warned him that although he would be the greatest chief of all time, he must beware of power, which did worse things to a man's mind than drinking or smoking *dagga*. "These you use little or not at all, my son," said the dying man faintly, "but power you seek for and drink deep. Mix it with mercy and the counsel of friends or it will drive you mad."

And Shaka grieved and begged Mbiya not to leave him, but the old man thanked him for all he had done, and said how good a son he had been and that he would try to visit him in his dreams from the land of the ancestors. And so he bade farewell and died, and Shaka saw to the arranging of his funeral. Some say that his spirit did indeed visit and advise Shaka in his later life.

Now Shaka did something that needed a new kind of courage. For it was said by the Nguni that evil could be used against a community through witches, whether these knew what they were doing or did not. Witchcraft and witchcraft alone was the answer to disasters, famine and illness, the killing strike of lightning. And there were witch doctors and diviners who in those days used to smell out a witch, snuffling and howling like sickening half-human hounds. Power was theirs, even against a chief, the power of abject fear. Most of them were women made hideous by too much belief in their own power. Every Zulu feared them; when a victim was smelled out, he was seized and killed in one of the filthiest ways imaginable and his whole family was killed with him. His cattle would be taken and some at least would go to the witch finders.

Who would be next for the smelling? Every man trembled and distrusted his neighbor. The unity of the clan was broken and the witch doctors and diviners became more important and powerful than the chief and his army. And yet everyone was so afraid of the unknown that they accepted the terror and cowered under it. But not so Shaka. He was determined to shield his own friends, after diviners went too far and smelled out Mgobozi, and also Mdlaka, one of his most loyal commanders. Shaka gave them sanctuary and declared to the people that, from this time on, any smelling-out of witchcraft must be confirmed by himself; all who were loyal to him, above all the army, were safe. All his people felt the terror lift; they need no longer be afraid of witchcraft. Shaka their father and leader had taken all upon himself. He, a young man, no longer bowed to ancient evil. So long as nothing, no disobedience or folly, came between him and them, they were safe. Later on he made a test which showed up to the whole people the falseness of the pretended divination.

But now there was war, most of all with Zwide of the Ndwandwe tribe. Dingiswayo had tried to come to terms both with him and with Matiwane of the Ngwane; he had tried to persuade them both to become part of a strong and orderly Nguni nation. But it was no use; they could not see his vision. And Dingiswayo would never let loose Shaka and his regiments, who could have crushed them. By now Shaka had begun the strict training of his men in regiments, the dreaded *impis*, each in a village of its own, living in strict discipline, unmarried, drilling relentlessly in the hot sun hour after hour, until they could charge all out in a straight line across the toughest country, then halt, shout with one voice, and stamp with the right foot in a single thunder.

But these men, who were being hammered into an invincible army, had to bear a merciless system of punishment. Those who failed or disobeyed were clubbed or speared. All that can be said is that, at about the same time, the discipline of the British Navy, into which men were press-ganged, was kept by constant and brutal floggings. This was the making of Nelson's ships of the line, just as the smashed Zulu skulls were the understructure of Shaka's armies.

Somehow Dingiswayo was lured into the hands of Zwide and his witch mother Ntombazi; it is said that this was due to strong magic. The executioner's spear pierced him, his head was cut off and hung with the rest in Ntombazi's hut. When Shaka and his men came, they came too late for anything but mourning for their wise chief and for the maidens who had gone with him to the fatal meeting and had stabbed themselves to the heart over his body. Dingiswayo's armies were in retreat, though many of his Mtetwa tribesmen joined Shaka, and so did his old friend Ngoboka of the Sokulu. But Zwide was determined to extend his power, to become the paramount chief as Dingiswayo had so nearly become, but by force, not by persuasion. One chief after another was killed and beheaded for Ntombazi's pleasure. Among them was Zwide's son-in-law Mashobane of the Amakumalo. But he had a son who was to be more famous than Zwide—this was Mzilikazi, the Path of Blood, who slipped away from his cruel grandfather and joined Shaka, who loved him and thought of him as a son.

Steadily Zwide grew more powerful. Other tribes hesitated as to whether to ally themselves with Zwide or Shaka. Then Zwide attacked. His army outnumbered Shaka's Zulus perhaps by two to one. Shaka's answer to this was something new in tactics; he withdrew all his men to Qokli Hill, knowing they would be surrounded, but with plenty of food and drink. In front there was a difficult ford at which many of Zwide's army were killed by the defenders. But more and more reinforcements came to join Zwide, so that he ended with a force so large that it seemed the Zulus must be overwhelmed. His heir, Nomahlanjana, was in command, and a good soldier. The Zulus on the hill kept themselves half hidden, but they had eaten and drunk well and were in good heart, for Shaka was with them, going from one group to another with orders and encouragement. Nomahlanjana's army attacked vigorously but fell into confusion, and the Zulus waiting for Shaka's word and in strict discipline charged suddenly downhill. There was close in-fighting; the stabbing spears of the Amazulus drank blood and again blood.

This kind of attack went on, but as the sun rose higher, the Ndwandwe grew more and more thirsty and had to go back to the river to drink, while the Zulus still had their water on the hill. All day the fighting raged on, but the Zulu discipline which Shaka had worked on for so long held, in spite of terrible losses. The fighting was the fiercest that had ever been seen among the Nguni; the dead were piled over one another. The Ndwandwe were as brave as the Zulus. They had been led by Nomahlanjana and the other princes, good fighters all, Zwide's pride and joy—but at the end of the day, where were they? Dead, all dead, and blood trickling down the hill, and with them hundreds of the bravest of the Zulus, for whom Shaka would mourn when the time came, but not yet, for the battle was still raging farther out beyond Qokli Hill. A day and a night of fighting, and the remains of Zwide's great army were in retreat, leaving thousands of dead. But almost half Shaka's army were killed or seriously wounded. He wept for them. Yet their reputation as fighters was now so great that other tribes began to come in of their own free will to join the Amazulu. The Mtetwa, without Dingiswayo, looked to Shaka, and soon it became hard to know whether a man belonged to one tribe or the other. They were Shaka's own army.

Would Shaka then become Dingiswayo's successor as builder of the Nguni nation? It seemed so. Gradually Shaka re-formed his army. Mgobozi, recovered from the wounds he had received on Qokli Hill, drilled new regiments of the incomers. A maidens' regiment was formed, the Vutwamini, which stayed in a separate war kraal and kept the same discipline as the men.

Yet Zwide also was remaking his armies, in bitter grief and mourning for his sons and unquenchable hatred of Shaka, whose domains were now extended from the small Zulu territory to overlordship of thousands of square miles of good land, forest and grazing, high ground and low ground. Shaka too was preparing new regiments, the young ones with black oxhide shields just touched with white, the best and bravest with shields like his own from the pure-white royal oxen. Shaka and his counselors were watching Zwide, constantly getting news of his armies, but they were also watching the white incomers, seaward and southward, and wondering what they were looking for and what danger they portended. They knew about, and hated, the Portuguese slave traders. Would these others be as bad?

In the break between wars Shaka held the great Umkosi, the harvest festival. This was a gathering of all the people, partly for rejoicing, for new songs and dancing, partly for politics, free speech and questioning, but partly also for magic to help the crops to grow. For the King, Shaka of the Amazulu, was the source of all well-being, father of crops and herds, father of the army, joiner-together of the past—the ancestors—and the future—the children yet unborn. Although he had broken the power of the evil witch diviners, he still kept his own war doctor to keep him safe from any magic that ill-wishers might aim at him and to see that his army was equally protected.

Who knows how much he believed in all this? He would not have been of his time without believing part of it.

The Umkosi was also the occasion for a great tribal meeting at which anyone could question their chief. This was a pattern of government among the Nguni and meant that there was always a possibility of face-to-face discussion between rulers and ruled, so long as the conventions of polite speech were kept to. This way justice was seen to be done and good sense upheld. Shaka might answer in a riddling way which could test the intelligence of his questioners, but this too was part of the enjoyment, when the Great Elephant, their father, met his sons.

There were feats of public courage to be undertaken, such as the capture and killing of the fierce black bull, part of the ritual for strengthening the army. There was dancing by the warriors, including the regiment of maidens, dressed in leafy girdles or sometimes with a small bead apron. A few daughters, perhaps of headmen, might have necklaces or bracelets, but for the rest the dark-brown, shining beauty of unflawed skin over softly strong muscles was clothing enough. They and the young men in their full war dress with the tossing plumes and flashing spears danced in long lines, hundreds, and when all the soldiers were in it together, thousands of them. All had bathed and dusted themselves with sweet-smelling leaves and Shaka himself danced in the midst among the sharp, heady smell of clean sweat and herbs.

His mother Nandi watched from a pile of rush mats on the top of a heaped mound where his sister Nomkoba and Pampata his love sat with the royal ladies. After all the days and years of misery, all these dancers and soldiers

100

were Nandi's; she was the most honorable, the Great She Elephant, Queen of the Amazulu. All her early sorrows were now made good.

Yet, before that, Shaka had also seen to the affairs of peace, to the crops. In the morning before dawn he had left his royal hut to the urgent singing summons of men and women; he was wearing corn ears and pieces of plants and herbs as well as magic beads. He walked, looking neither to right nor to left, until he came to the gate of the great cattle kraal. In his mouth he held bitter-tasting water in which medicines from plants or animals had been steeped and this he squirted out toward the rising sun and over a fire which had been kindled from special wood. In this way it was said he would keep away disease and evil spirits.

There were also visits to the ancestral burial ground and invocation of the ancestors, for they too must be part of the rejoicing and preparation for the future. That year there was an ample grain harvest, and most of it, on Shaka's orders, was stored in deep and secret caves. The grain would have been sorghum and perhaps millet, though it is possible that already a little maize was grown. This had come from South America some two centuries earlier and might have been grown near the Portuguese seaports on the east coast of Africa, or even at the Cape; an adventurous Zulu might have brought back a few grains and planted them. We do not know. But when crops are women's work, and women do not travel, they do not alter much.

Zwide's armies were about to move at the beginning of the winter. The time for war was after harvest, when the men grew impatient and colder weather made long marches easier. Shaka was determined that his enemies should find nothing to eat, so not only was the corn taken away but he ordered all cattle, sheep, and goats, and all women and children to leave their kraals and go into hiding in the forests. They went easily, carrying pots and bedding on their heads, and knew they would be guarded against enemies and wild beasts. And then the Ndwandwe army came shouting in, not now under King Zwide's sons, but under Soshangane, who was later to lead another army to found the Shangaan empire, driving the Portuguese out of most of the territory they claimed south of the Zambesi. There were some 18,000 of them, better trained and disciplined now, but still wearing their heavy sandals, though many by this time had stabbing blades on their spears. They found little or nothing to eat in the Zulu country which they invaded, nothing but empty huts and empty cattle kraals.

The Ndwandwe army was lured on, sometimes by pretended retreat. They were now on the edge of the forest, and inside it, camped under the enormous trees, was Shaka, making his plans with his generals, among them the young and splendid Mzilikazi, hating Zwide his grandfather, who had killed his father. Everything was kept hidden till the last: less chance of news getting to the enemy. Then Shaka found a plan to put panic into the Ndwandwe by sending parties of his men in at night after the campfires had fallen to embers, crawling like snakes to stab their enemies, who would think themselves attacked by witches, since it was no Nguni custom to fight this way. Then the Ndwandwe would retreat in bad order.

So indeed it went. All had been carefully worked out with a system of passwords; some of the bravest of the Zulus stayed all night in the Ndwandwe camp, killing and clubbing, and most of them came back safe. After a sleepless night and little food, the Ndwandwe were in retreat. But Soshangane was a general of Shaka's own ability and the Ndwandwe army still outnumbered the Zulus by half as much again. The Zulus caught up with the retreating Ndwandwe by mid-morning, and battle began with the usual forming up of the two armies half a mile apart. But Shaka gained an initial victory by cutting off the two ends of Soshangane's wings, though at the cost of terrible losses among his own regiments. The main armies never engaged, but when Soshangane began his retreat the Zulus harassed him and he still had little food for his men.

Yet most of the northern army was still there, outnumbering the Zulus, and until the Ndwandwe were completely defeated, the war would go on and the Zulus would be in peril. Shaka watched for a chance to attack and at last found it at the fording of a river where Soshangane had allowed his formation to thin out. The Zulu *impis* came down over a hill brow, keeping time and perfect contact with the war chant that held them together terrifyingly until the moment before the *si-gi-di* scream of the final charge.

The Ndwandwe had fought well, but half were killed and half had lost their shields and weapons when they were forced into the river. The Ndwandwe picked regiment which was covering the ford fought desperately, losing almost every man, and stopped the Zulus from attacking the ford. There was death and wounding, the shields hooked, the spears into the heart, the fury of men all out to kill, all along the bends and shallows of the river, with the Ndwandwe re-forming and the Zulus raging and attempting to follow. But at last the Zulus began to get a footing on the far side and to press the Ndwandwe armies, but away from their direct road home.

Suddenly the way was open. Shaka sent his two freshest regiments to capture Zwide and his witch mother before they heard the news. They made the seventy miles in a cross-country run and sang the Ndwandwe victory song as they came to the royal kraal. Everyone rushed out to welcome them, but they started killing too soon and the King escaped, though his mother the witch queen was captured. And now the Zulu army was pouring into the country of the Ndwandwe, killing and killing—old men, women, and children—burning every hut, driving off every cow, sheep, or goat. There was no mercy. This time it was to be over once and for all.

Only a small remnant of Zwide's army escaped, with Soshangane still in command, but they could do nothing. Shaka's victory was complete. He finished it off by rewarding the army, distributing cattle, and giving special awards to the bravest and cleverest. He also did something which had never been thought of before: he gave cattle generously to the families of the dead warriors. For almost half the army had been killed. This thought for the widows and children and aged parents was new, and so was the way in which he gave the best of the cattle to the common warriors, picking out the cows and oxen himself in a day of rewards and feasting and song. Here the makers of praises, using the traditional words but stringing them newly, adding a fresh glitter of similes, rewarded the deeds of the best of the fighters in something nobler than cattle. And the excitement and delight at being praised and of belonging to Shaka, their King but now overlord of lands far beyond their thoughts, pulsed with singing joy through the heart of every warrior, putting out the pain of wounds or the loss of friends. This was victory. This was Shaka.

Ntombazi the witch was doomed. She had boasted, to terrify people, that she rode a hyena through the night and had absolute power over these fearful beasts. Yes, she even boasted of this to Shaka when she stood before him for judgment. So things were done to her this-wise. She was shut into her hut, where the skulls of the chiefs whom she and Zwide had captured and killed grinned from the walls, and with her was put a live, huge, and hungry hyena. In the screaming and cracking of bones her boasts were shown to be empty.

From now on, there was a time of rejoicing. Many fighters were promoted to the headring of the honored man, who is ready to marry and set up a household. Mgobozi's wives mostly had babies on their backs, fat and strong. There was meat and beer, dancing and singing. Shaka was now the overlord of all the eastern Nguni between the Tugela River north to the Pongola River and far inland. Dingiswayo had never had such an empire. There was a great hunt; Shaka was always at the most exciting and dangerous place. It ended with piles of leopard skins and elephant tusks and awards and praises to the slayers: praises, too, for those who had met their death on the horns of the buffalo or by the jaws of the lion.

But Shaka, who had started his life as a despised and wretched child, was now absolute lord of the Zulu nation and knew in his own mind that there were further conquests ahead of him and that he would always win—what would he become? Perhaps Pampata tried to warn him, to tell him that the tallest tree is the one to be stricken by lightning, or that when the lion roars too loudly the other animals of the forest band together and in the end take him in a pit. Perhaps he would listen to her for a while and then become lost in dreams of greatness and power and blood. He would be aware that he was utterly Zulu, heaven itself, that he had rained death already on thousands, men, women, and children, who had somehow been in the way of that Zulu thought and substance which he held in his mind, and that he would kill many more. His fate was strongly upon him.

And then? Absolute power did destroy Shaka as a person, in the way it destroys everybody. He became terrified of getting old and frantically tried to stave it off. He became jealous of younger men. Yet he refused to take the consolations of age, the wives and children. When a few white people did at last go as far inland as Shaka's court, he received them in a friendly and trusting way, but hoped that, among the many other magic things which they seemed to have, there would be one magic against old age. When in the end his mother died, he seems really to have gone mad for a time and hit out, killing his own people. A king with less power might have struck but could have been stopped from actual killing. Nobody stopped Shaka.
He went on conquering, so that his armies were dreaded,

and wise men like Moshesh of Lesotho, even when unconquered, would send him at least a nominal tribute. But it
was violence and killing all the time, so that, although they
knew that he was the greatest ruler they had ever had, he
began to lose the love and trust of his people as a whole.
He became feared by many, hated by a few. In the end he
was stabbed to death, perhaps among others by his half
brother, Dingaan. But before he died he prophesied that
the white men coming in from the sea would now be able
to conquer Zululand.

For more about Shaka there is a very readable book,
Shaka Zulu *by Conrad Ritter, published by Longmans,
Green & Co Ltd, London.*

After his death, Dingaan was King of Zululand, but by
now the Dutch farmers from the Cape were trekking north,
each wanting a huge bit of land for his own cattle. At the
same time there was pressure from the English coming
into Natal. There was constant war, ending in the battle
of Blood River, when the Dutch destroyed most of Dingaan's impis. It looked as though Shaka's prophecy was
coming true. And it was passed from one person to another.
Even the small boy, Cetshwayo, Shaka's nephew, must
have heard it and wondered. Meanwhile Zwide's former
general, Soshangane, had gone north and founded the
Shangaan empire. Sobhuza, another Nguni general,
founded what is now Swaziland. Long before Shaka died,
Mzilikazi broke away westward for an immense trail of
conquest, driving the Tswana peoples and finally settling
around the royal town of Bulawayo. Shaka never caught
up with him or destroyed him, as probably he might have
done. Why not? Was Mzilikazi so much like the son that

107

Shaka refused to have? Were the natural feelings of fatherhood so strong that even the King of the Zulus could not avoid them? There are things in the heart which even the greatest conqueror cannot fight.

7 The Mountain of the Night

The rivers rise high in the mountains; they leap down the scarps into deep glens among tall and shady trees where birds nest and flutter, then wind on into level land, wonderful grazing ground, rich land for crops, a wholly desirable country.

Here were villages neatly kept and clean, the cone-shaped, thatched roofs melting into the landscape. Nobody would have wanted to build a proud demanding house which stuck out and proclaimed itself. But houses could and should be decorated with patterns in plaster or stones. Where the land was generous, there were plenty of villages; children were fat; there was milk and meat.

Across the green valley there would be another village, its brown thatch melting into the brown cliffs. Above the cliffs rose a high mountain. There were grazing tablelands to which the cattle could be driven in case of attack, the way blocked with boulders, so that any attackers would be speared or shot with arrows from above. There were times when this was bound to happen. But it did not matter very much if a few houses were burned; they were easily built again. With luck, the invaders might miss the buried grain.

There was such a village which had a strange chief; indeed, he had more than one village and in the villages were many houses, some built rather differently, with another trick of thatching or decorating. The pots standing at the door were not quite like the pots elsewhere. People knew that this was sometimes because the hut belonged to one of the new wives the chief had brought back from his wanderings, or more simply, these huts had been built by people from other tribes, even those who had been long thought of as enemies but who had now been accepted as friends.

For indeed Motlomi was a strange chief. People came to him for help in their disputes with others or in their disputes with spirits and ill-wishers. He was skilled with herbs and could cure many kinds of illness, refusing to allow the ideas of witchcraft; but he was still more adept at curing quarrels and stopping bloodshed. He could forgive wrongs done to him and he did not wish to be a war leader. He drank only water or milk. Many honored him for his skill in rainmaking, but he smiled even at that, because he was forever wondering about the causes of things, asking questions to which nobody knew the answer.

Many men came and sat on the spread skin at Motlomi's feet and listened to his wisdom, and one of these was a boy from a small tribe who was perhaps related to him, though not very closely. He was a lively lad who had been nicknamed Moshesh, the Shaver-off, because of the daring and clever way he had shaved off all the cattle of a powerful chief. But Moshesh was more than a young bandit, and Motlomi, questioning him, knew this, and taking off one of his long, golden earrings, he put it onto the ear of Moshesh, saying that this was a sign of rule, and he would rule many men, but only if he understood them and gave them the three things which men need most: freedom, justice, and peace.

And Moshesh thought carefully of the words he had heard from old Motlomi and he began to know that killing and cattle raiding were not the noblest things for a man to do, but he must think far ahead and stop quarrels before they began to harm people and happiness. The years went by, and by now he was a young leader, married, chief of a small tribe, sometimes at peace but more often having to take refuge from raiders, some army on the move, perhaps Mzilikazi's Zulus, perhaps the Batlokwa under Queen Mmantatisi. War. It was always war. Always on the alert, always risking men's lives and the carrying off of cattle and women. Always fear lest the enemy destroy all the crops for next year's food. War. The sharpening of the spears. The songs. The skill. Yes, war was a pleasure, the greatest, the height of excitement, the point of danger, and

111

yet—was this all there was to it? Had not the old man, Motlomi, spoken of other ways of ruling, other ways of being a chief?

Without being in any sense conquered, Moshesh had thought it wiser to send a tribute of cranes' feathers and other decorations to King Shaka, and this stood him in good stead when he was attacked by one of the other Nguni tribes. He sent a messenger to say how sad he was that he could not send his tribute, but this other tribe lay between him and his overlord. Shaka immediately attacked and Moshesh was saved with little trouble to himself. This was worth a few feathers.

At first Moshesh had a stronghold on Buthe Buthe, but this hilltop was not secure enough and Moshesh decided to move with his small tribe, the beginnings of the Basuto people, to a much stronger mountain top, Thaba Bosiu, the Mountain of the Night. It was a difficult march. His band of men and women, driving their cattle before them, were going through cannibal country. One of those who fell by the roadside and was killed and eaten was Moshesh's grandfather, Peete. When his people had settled down and were strong again, they wanted above all to avenge themselves on the cannibals. But Moshesh managed to persuade them that these cannibals were indeed the living tombs of their victims, including his own ancestor, and could be suitably purified. This policy was so successful that in a short while the cannibals settled down to be among his most peaceable and loyal supporters and followers.

These eaters of human flesh, who had probably learned the custom from the wild people in the north, did not, perhaps, do it deliberately, but were driven by sheer hunger when they had been robbed in war of everything else. Later, even Moshesh admitted it, saying, "It was we, the masters of this country, who drove you to live on human flesh, for men cannot eat stones. You ate my father, but before that, I had eaten yours." And he meant to say by this that his people had taken the others' crops and cattle and everything else. He ended by saying, "Let it all be forgotten!"

For indeed there was so much killing to forget. The Zulu armies, first of Shaka, then of Mzilikazi, Soshangane, and the rest, were so thoroughly trained as war machines that they could not stop; they had to go on and on and conquer and destroy. Others, flying from them, fell on still more remote, peaceable neighbors. This is what people mean by the *Mfecane,* the time of troubles. It seemed as though there would be no end to it: conquest and later on revenge, conquest and revenge. Something had to be done. Some new way of thought and action must come into being. This was the message from the dead, the wise old man Motlomi.

Queen Mmantatisi's proud and violent son, Sekonyela, chief of the Batlokwa, whom Moshesh had been trying to conciliate, going so far as to ask him to take charge of the initiation house where his son and other young men were being circumcised and at the same time learning the wisdom of the ancestors, broke his promise of friendship. Moshesh was away on a cattle raid and Sekonyela took the opportunity of attacking Thaba Bosiu, killing and looting and burning the initiation house. He had even carried off Mamohato, the Great Wife of Moshesh, though in a coun-

113

ter-attack she saved herself from the Batlokwa who had hold of her. Moshesh came back to hear of this treachery; he saw the burned house, though his son Letsie and the other young men had saved their cows and driven off the looters. What was he to do? What would Motlomi have advised? He sent four head of his captured cattle to Sekonyela, but asked him from whence came the fire that burned the initiation house? How did it come that his people had been killed? What answer could Sekonyela give? And it is said that Chief Sekonyela, for once in his life, was overcome with shame, and after this he left the Basuto alone.

But the lands of the Basuto people were always a temptation to would-be conquerors. Thaba Bosiu stood a little way from the main mountain ranges; all round it were green valleys and water. But it was easy enough for the people of the valleys to drive their cattle up if an enemy came. The women, looking back, would weep and lament to see their houses in flames, but they were carrying their babies on their backs and most of their household goods on their heads. All would be rebuilt. But this meant that nobody could have anything belonging to them which was very heavy or durable. They must be able to carry whatever they treasured up to the Mountain of the Night. And this mountain top was virtually impregnable; when Mzilikazi sent an army of his Ndebele tribesmen to attack and take it, the defenders threw stones and hurled spears down the narrow passes. It was all very well for the *indunas* in command of the Ndebele regiments to tear the ostrich plumes from their soldiers' heads and trample them underfoot. The Mountain of the Night could not be taken. Moshesh followed it up in a way that would have made Motlomi proud of his pupil. He sent some oxen over to the defeated and wounded Ndebele and a message in the mouths of the herdsmen to say: "Our master thinks you must have been hungry to attack his people. He sends you these oxen; you must eat and go in peace." And so they did, and never attacked him again.

By now, more and more people were gathering in around the Mountain of the Night, feeling that here they would have protection and peace. Men who had been working on the white farms in the Cape left with their families, driving the cattle they had bought out of their wages. Moshesh welcomed and settled them in villages. There were little groups from one tribe or another. They had to be fed; and sometimes Moshesh or his brothers went cattle-raiding themselves, down into the plains; not too often, but enough for people to know he was a power. But also there were brigands, Griqua and Kosana, armed with guns. These were mixed Dutch and Hottentot people, quick and fierce and without the order or restraint of the settled Bantu tribes. Most of them were mounted and it was from them that Moshesh's people, who by now would have thought of themselves as the Basuto nation, learned to ride, soon becoming a nation of horsemen, more and more often armed with guns. Moshesh was a family man before he tried riding the first horse which was brought to him, with a wooden bit and a grass bridle, and until he got the knack of it he balanced himself with two long sticks. But soon he became a keen rider and bought or took as gifts as many horses as he could. The Basuto bred and trained the ponies into extraordinary cleverness, so that

115

they could find their way up and down mountain paths and would answer to the least inclination of their riders. Even today Lesotho (the name of the country, which before independence in 1967 was Basutoland—it means the same thing) is gay with horsemen, mostly wearing the colored blankets which drape like the riders' cloaks on ancient Greek vases; today, too, one sees women and girls riding and it will be long enough before the mountain tracks will take anything but a Basuto pony.

As the years went on, more and more people came to Lesotho, putting themselves under the wise rule of Moshesh. When people were in trouble—and trouble often meant having nothing to eat, not even a few handfuls of grass seed or a rock rabbit they had managed to snare—they came for help to Moshesh, and mostly got it. Among those he protected were the grandchildren of Motlomi, fallen on hard times. But now there was another kind of newcomer, white men with long, big-wheeled ox wagons like moving houses, in which they kept their women and children. They did not come peaceably but would chase away, sometimes shoot, those who came near their cattle. What kind were they? How did they come to have these reddish faces sprouting bushes of hair? Their women too had long hair of a color like flowers and wrapped themselves entirely in cloth—why? Moshesh recollected all he had heard of them and he became uneasy.

It was about this time that a wandering Griqua came to Moshesh in the Mountain of the Night. His name was Adam Krotz and his grandfather was Dutch. He was a Christian and had lived in the mission village of Philippolis, where the Paris Evangelical Mission had its headquarters among the Griquas. He was able to answer many of the questions that Chief Moshesh asked him about the white people. They talked far into the night. When the fire began to die down, someone would throw on an armful of brushwood. The sparks floated up toward the stars, and Adam Krotz spoke to Moshesh about his God, high, high up, who called the souls of men. But also he spoke to him about the mission schools and the skill of the missionaries, who could heal sicknesses and pains, and had answers for all questions.

Moshesh thought about this and above all he thought that if he could get some of these missionaries to come to his country, they would speak to the white men in the wagons and stop them from shooting his people. It would appear that white would only obey white, and if so, one must have some whites on one's side. It would be well, too, to have schools, where young boys would perhaps learn some of the things which white men knew, such as healing. So he decided to send cattle to these strangers and invite them to his country.

It was in 1833 that a party of French missionaries arrived in Philippolis meaning to go and work among the Bahurutse toward the west; but things were completely unsettled there. Mzilikazi had not yet found the place where he wanted to make his home, and his armies were on the move, raiding and burning and killing. It did not appear as though mission work were possible in that direction. Fathers Casalis, Arbousset, and Gosselin were discussing this and wondering what to do, praying for guidance,

117

when messengers came to them. The interpreters explained that these men came in peace from Chief Moshesh of Thaba Bosiu, the head of the Basuto nation, and that they had started with a gift of cattle from him, but the Griquas had stolen them. Although they came empty-handed, their hearts were full, and the message of their chief was that the white missionaries should come and live with him.

What sort of man was this Chief Moshesh, Father Casalis asked. Adam Krotz and others answered. All he heard was favorable. This was the answer to prayer. The missionaries told the messengers that they would come, and sent them back to Lesotho with gifts for their king.

Moshesh met them with expressions of delight and helped them to find a suitable place for their mission, in a sheltered and pleasant valley, which they called Morija. This was in July, the middle of the southern African winter, with snow on the mountains, but they could see how gardens and planted trees would flourish at Morija. Moshesh sent his eldest son, Letsie, with some of his age mates, to help the three French missionaries to build themselves a house.

Moshesh was by then a man in his forties, tall and noble-looking, with sensitive, artist's fingers that could yet hurl a spear; he lived a temperate life, avoiding alcohol, tobacco, and even snuff. He had some forty wives, many of whom had been married on diplomatic grounds; and if a chief married a wife from far off, it was kinder to marry two sisters, who would be company for each other until they made friends with the rest. Moshesh loved small children and spent much time with them, and much too with the older men, questioning and digging into their wisdom. In his young days he would wear a feathered headband, earrings and necklaces, bracelets of copper and ivory; he might carry a royal cloak of leopard skin dressed so that it was light and soft as silk. Later on, he was induced to wear the heavy and inappropriate European clothes and even a top hat, but that was not how the missionaries saw him when he welcomed them to Lesotho. Like Motlomi, his father in wisdom, he wanted always to know more, and soon he was questioning the missionaries, though he did not always accept everything they said. But he was determined to protect them, and a good relationship grew up, in which each party trusted the other. This was to stand the Basuto in good stead in later times. The Paris Evangelical Mission was always wholeheartedly on their side.

It was quite soon after the missionaries settled in that Moshesh had news of a white man sent by the Governor of the Cape, the headman of the Great White King (soon to be succeeded by the Great White Queen, Victoria), who was visiting the chiefs along the Caledon River, as well as Mzilikazi himself. There was talk of treaties, and later treaties were indeed made, though with still another set of whites, the Dutch with the ox wagons, who were beginning to build themselves villages. How was one to tell which of these whites was the best to have as an ally? The wisdom of the old men was useless here.

King Moshesh consulted his missionaries, who were the happier to help him because a rival mission, the Wesleyans, had settled in the lower part of the Caledon

Valley. They had asked leave of Moshesh and Sekonyela; they had prepared elaborate legal documents and then claimed that the land belonged to them and that their followers, nominal Christians, could set up as independent chiefs. This was, of course, in complete contradiction to customary Bantu law. Land was not something you could buy or sell; nor were the few cattle and sheep which the Wesleyans had handed over a fair price in anyone's eyes for hundreds of square miles of land! Doubtless Father Casalis rubbed it into Moshesh that if only he had been able to read he would not have put his mark to this agreement. But meanwhile the Paris Evangelical Mission told the Wesleyans that there had been no transfer of land, only the right to cultivate and build, and that all were within the kingdom of Moshesh.

Now began the direct contact with the British at the Cape. No doubt the missionaries of Morija did the actual writing, but they did not hide from Moshesh what they had written. It was also the beginning of the very clear understanding by the King of Lesotho that he had to deal with two sets of whites and that it might be well to play one against the other. Moshesh decided that he would assist the British as their friend and ally and keep order for them within his kingdom, in return getting guns and ammunition and some assistance in his just claim to the Caledon lands. Soon afterward he decided to have three of his sons educated at the Cape, in care of the Governor. However, he did his very best to keep on good terms with the Dutch, who were nearer.

In the years following, Moshesh was caught between the

Dutch—the Boer farmers, always with their eyes on his green valleys, who were there on his borders with their guns at the ready—and the British government emissaries with their civil or military titles who dashed up and down between Cape Town and the Mountain of the Night, wearing handsome uniforms and riding splendid and enviable horses. Nor had Sekonyela of the Batlokwa ever quite abandoned his ambitions; he looked enviously at Thaba Bosiu. Moshesh's own sons did not make things any easier: they were young; they wanted to fight and rule. They did not agree with their father's peaceful ideas.

The disagreement about the boundary line went on year after year; promises of settlements were made, and then broken by impatient young men. Again, a hill or a river might be known to one side under a Boer name, while the other knew it only by its name in Sesotho, the language of the Basuto. It is likely enough that quarrels between one tribe or another were encouraged by both English- and Dutch-speaking whites: let them kill and weaken one another. All the better for the Europeans!

Cattle were raided and sometimes Moshesh was blamed for something which he himself disapproved of. There came a point when the British government decided to fine him 6,000 good cattle and 300 horses for alleged theft and depredations. They only gave him ten days to collect them and meanwhile began to mass troops along the border. Moshesh not only put out diplomatic feelers toward the Dutch but also managed to break up a regiment of Barolong which the British had taken on to their side, killing a number of them. The British had to fall back, blaming everyone but their own policymakers. But Moshesh knew this could not last; he must build up alliances quickly with the other whites.

There were letters and meetings; at one point it seemed that the British officials admitted their government had been in the wrong. But they were recalled; others took their place. Moshesh felt he could trust no white except perhaps his own missionaries. He must have wondered if some day they would betray him, not foreseeing the trouble they would run into later on, when he was an old man, for being too much on the African side. Meanwhile, he must strengthen himself. Above all, he must have the trained horses, the war beasts.

He married some of his daughters to chiefs whom he wished to be on good terms with. Two sisters went to Chief Kgamanyane of the Bakgatla. As for his sons, he sent some to be baptized and educated European-fashion with whatever thoughts and new ways of doing things might come from that, but others were initiated in the old way and educated for courage and cunning and quick decision. Two sets of gods or powers might be placated. Two sets of opinion in Lesotho would approve one action or the other.

The British were beginning to feel that Basutoland must be brought into line; the old man up there on the Mountain of the Night was a menace, or might be. The new Governor at the Cape, General Sir George Cathcart, collected a large force, including such of the Royal Artillery as would be necessary for shelling him out of his stronghold. This would be used unless the fine, which by now had been increased to 10,000 head of cattle and 1,000 horses, was immediately paid.

122

Sir George demanded that Moshesh should come personally to see him and under the eyes of his soldiers and noses of his cannon accept the terms. The Caledon River rose in flood, one of those devastating African floods, when in a few hours a peaceful, sluggish river tears everything away, spreads far over its banks with the brown, menacing water full of uprooted trees, dead beasts, anything it has caught. Moshesh could not cross, but two of his sons managed to swim the flood. Sir George would not even receive them.

However, the flood went down as quickly as it had risen. Moshesh and the Governor met. The interview is on record. Moshesh asked only for more time: how was he to get all those cattle out of his people? The Governor said: "If you are not able to collect them, I must go and do it; and if any resistance is made, it will then be war and I shall not be satisfied with 10,000 head but shall take all I can."

To this, King Moshesh answered: "Do not talk of war! For however anxious I may be to avoid it, you know that a dog when beaten will show his teeth."

Under further pressure, Moshesh answered that like everyone else he had thieves among his people. The Governor told him that he must catch the thieves and bring them. "I will hang them."

Moshesh answered, shocked: "I do not wish you to hang them but to talk to them and give them advice. If you hang them, they cannot talk." That would be the Bantu way in a court of justice. Wrongdoers were not simply to be punished out of hand; they must be shown the error of their ways and brought back within the moral order of the tribe.

123

But the Governor gave a tough answer. "If I hang them, they cannot steal, and I am not going to talk any more." Three days, and if Moshesh had not got the cattle, it would be war.

On the third day, one of his sons brought in to the English camp 3,500 head of cattle, all that could be collected in the time. Presumably General Sir George Cathcart supposed that King Moshesh was a kind of storybook tyrant who could just take his subjects' cattle. In reality, he could not possibly have done so, even if he had felt it right, which he did not. To make matters worse, the British had now given arms and ammunition to the old enemy, Sekonyela of the Batlokwa.

The invasion of Lesotho began. General Cathcart and his forces marched straight on toward Thaba Bosiu. But several of his columns were ambushed. Some of his soldiers were killed with lances captured from English lancers who had underrated their opponents and now lay dead and stripped. It was then that Moshesh sent a letter formally acknowledging defeat and begging not to be considered an enemy to the Queen. General Cathcart welcomed this letter as his letout and withdrew his armies, though affecting to speak as the higher authority making terms. But King Moshesh knew that in fact he himself had won and that the whites would never forgive him; in their eyes, the blacks must always be the losers, the punished. Sooner or later, the vengeance of the whites would come if he did not make his victory look like something else. It was a decision he had to make alone, for his counselors would not realize the hard truth. Hence the letter, written at midnight by his educated son, Nehemiah, helped by Father Casalis. Yet, how would his own fighters take it? He knew that the days were over when a young man must go out and wet his spear in blood before he was accepted as husband or householder. These were the times Motlomi had foreseen. But how many others even of his own family understood that?

Peace of an uneasy kind went on for some years, but when Sekonyela began again on his raiding tactics, Moshesh struck hard, taking up the war spear in his own hands and leading one of the parties. Sekonyela himself escaped, but his hill fort, almost as impregnable as Thaba Bosiu, was stormed. Moshesh offered him land as his vassal, but Sekonyela refused. In the end, the British gave him a farm; he retired there and died.

But boundary trouble went on. It did not help the Africans that the British government far off in London was not interested in spending effort or money on the affairs of southern Africa and that the Boer states were becoming stronger and more demanding. The trekkers with the wagons supposed themselves to be the Chosen of God and any land they wanted—such as the green Caledon Valley —was the Promised Land. Whoever kept them out of it was acting unscripturally. On top of this, land speculators had moved in and often what they speculated in was land which belonged to an African tribe. Moshesh's brother, Paulus Moperi, saw this clearly when he said; "The farmers want war; let them have it; but I will tell you beforehand it is not we that wish for it. The farmers long for it because their children are growing up and want farms in our country and think they will be able to get themselves immense herds of cattle." Yet Moshesh was always eager for settlement and peace.

It seemed more and more impossible. Whenever things were going well, either there would be cattle raiding by one of his young men, perhaps one of his own family, or there would be some Boer farmer settling across the boundary line, which never seemed to be agreed on by both sides. One must always prepare for war but, as King Moshesh grew older, he longed to be able to think about peace and to make the kind of laws which would fit a peaceful country. It was a long time ago that he had been a young man, a cattle raider himself. Now he wanted other things. Some were the same things the missionaries wanted; only the framework in which they were to be had was different. When he himself was, like the wise man Motlomi, an ancestor joined to his dead forefathers, how would people think of him? They would surely think of him as the joiner-together of tribes. They would think of him as the King of the Mountain of the Night. Would they think of him also as the maker and keeper of peace?

The time came when Moshesh, an old man, thought it best to ask that Lesotho should become a protectorate. He appealed to the White Queen and was accepted. In this way he saved the Basuto nation, though not all their land. Some of the best of it was in the end taken by the Transvaal Republic. Lesotho today is an independent country, but because only the mountains and valleys and difficult country were left to them after the voortrekkers had taken what they wanted, most of the men have to go and work

126

elsewhere. But they remember Moshesh and make poems and songs about him.

The next story happens a few hundred miles farther west. When Kgamanyane was born, Moshesh was already a successful young chief.

8 Kgamanyane of the Bakgatla

The bushes in front of his hide rustled. It was only a ledge in the rock, but he could go no farther. The wound from a Ndebele spear coming under his shield had made a deep gash in his leg. For all he knew, this was Mzilikazi's men hunting for him. And then it would be the end, for him and for the baby. His son, his eldest son. Pilane, Chief of the Bakgatla, reached behind him to the soft warmth of the sleeping baby. Let him not wake!

The bushes parted; it was all right, it was she. It was Mankube, and oh, she had food! Two light steps and she was in his arms, his beautiful loving wife, Mankube of the Batlokwa. "I found a kind goat," she said, "and I have milk for my lord—see!" She held it to his mouth. Her skin bag was full of roots; she started to pare them. "You are stronger," she said. "Tonight we must move. I could see smoke."

"It shall be as you say, my wife," said Pilane. And then, "I have longed to see you, Kgamanyane and I, we have longed!" For now she had picked up their son and was suckling him. For a moment it seemed to Pilane strange that he should be so close to a woman with a little baby; she should have been safe in her hut, among the women. But when Mzilikazi's fighters came, she had fled with him. All last night they had traveled together; he had leaned on her shoulder more and more as the stars wheeled and the wound in his leg stiffened. And she, with the baby on her back in his soft cradle of skins, had taken his war ax in her other hand, so that he could walk more easily. Whatever other wives he might have to marry, Mankube would always be his own, his Great Wife, as part of himself as his heart. And this son of his, Kgamanyane, he would always be the closest of his children.

And so it was. But there were other wives and other sons, and after Pilane died, there were quarrels about the succession. By that time the Bakgatla were strong again, a tribe to be reckoned with. The Ndebele had gone north, though not until, in one raid, they had captured three of Pilane's sons, including young Kgamanyane. But they were released, and helped in some of the peacemaking activities of Pilane, who was well thought of as a restorer of order and was a friend of many tribes, until in the end he too became an ancestor.

Kgamanyane had made his village at Moruleng, where

the beautiful morula trees lifted their heavy gray trunks into a canopy of green shade and every autumn shed a carpet of golden-green fruit for the children to gather up, rolling them onto a stone to soften the hard outer skin and get a delicious mouthful of sharp, scented pulp. He too had married many wives, but Dikolo, the mother of Linchwe and Ramono, was his Great Wife, and she was like a kind elder sister to the younger wives. How happily they lived together at Moruleng!

In the day Kgamanyane went hunting, for there were great herds of antelope all around, the best of food. But sometimes word came that a lion or a leopard had taken one of the cows. Then came the more dangerous hunting which tested a man. Indeed, a chief of the Bakgatla was not really a chief until he had killed his lion. Often Kgamanyane walked many miles to see his cattle, his many beautiful cattle grazing and fattening. In the evening there were fires and feasting; the wives would have made beer and porridge. Under the arch of stars there were songs and dancing and the telling of famous deeds. He, Kgamanyane, who was also Kgabo, which is to say either the little monkey or the quick flame of fire, would be one with his ancestors as with his sons.

But the happiness was not to last. By 1860 there were many Boer farmers coming in, and they made extraordinary claims. They said that all the land was theirs. They also said that the people who lived on the land and who had grazed their cattle there and raised their crops for longer than anyone could remember were their subjects. They must pay tax in the money of the white people, and this money they could only get by working for them. But there was something worse. The Bakgatla must provide men and women, boys and girls, to work without pay on the Boer farms or fight their wars for them—equally without pay—against other tribes. The Boers said that the young ones were apprentices, that they would learn to farm in the way of the whites. But they were taught nothing except sometimes to pray to the white god in words that they did not understand; and if they forgot the words, they were beaten.

They were beaten for much else. They were made to work day after day even in the hot time when all men stop work and sleep. When the oxen of the Boer farmers died, who pulled the plow? Boys who had been given to the farmers as apprentices, and they felt the ox whip on their shoulders. Paul Kruger was the leader of the Boers; at first Chief Kgamanyane had welcomed him and had helped him with his plowing and harvesting, sending men of his own regiment, the Masoso. He was sorry for the Boers at first; coming one family at a time, surely they must be poor people. He had given them cattle. Indeed, he had given them more cattle later, when this Kruger had told them that they, the Bakgatla, must buy the land. This seemed very strange, for it was the land on which they lived and where they pastured their cattle, but Kruger and his friends had guns which killed from far off and it seemed better to do what they wanted. Yet, in spite of that, after a while it was said that these cattle were not payment but a tribute and that the Boers were the owners of the land.

So many farmers settled that the Bakgatla found it hard to know where their cattle could go. These farmers were not content with the land around their houses and the gardens they could plant; they said that all the land was theirs, and they killed those who crossed their boundaries. And always, always, they were asking for more. Chief Kgamanyane did not know what to do. He did not want to quarrel with the Boers, any more than a man without a spear looks for a quarrel with a lion. He took his men to help the Boers against their enemies. But when they marched against Moshesh, at Thaba Bosiu, it was something different. He was married to two of Moshesh's daughters—when a wife came from far off, she would not be lonely if her sister came too. So, when it came to a battle, his men and the Basuto must appear to fight, but that would be all.

Kgamanyane made a praise song about himself; "I am a double-sharp-pointed awl that pricks both the cloak and the man that sews it, the nimble one. I was on this side, then I joined that; I used to be a red-skinned Boer. I have become a man of the Sotho, the famed one, son-in-law of Moshesh and eater of the people's gifts; on one leg I wear a trouser, on the other leg a kilt. I shot into the blackest darkness, I do not know if I hit, nor do I know if I missed. The spark burns those basking by the fire, it never burns those who stay away." And so he warned the Basuto not to be there when he attacked. This was a thing that the Boers did not find out, because they did not understand the ways of honor.

By now it was nine years later and there were more Boers, and more. And they kept asking for land and for apprentices; a man must be careful that his little son or grandson did not take the cattle near the land which these men claimed, for he might be shot or he might be caught and made a slave. In return, the Boers sometimes gave presents to the chief men of the tribe, perhaps guns or food for the guns, or perhaps this drink of theirs which made men feel full of greatness, but also of foolishness. But all were uneasy.

Kgamanyane called a *pitso*, a great meeting of all the men of the tribe, and these matters were talked over for a long time. Kgamanyane was angry; he tossed his head like a wild boar, and indeed there had been a song made, telling the Boers to keep their dogs away from the great boar, and by this they meant Kgamanyane. His brother Kgari was there too; he was a rainmaker, but yet he had begun to be uncertain of what he was doing. He had been listening to the missionaries, and if it was true that their god was above everything, how could he in the old way and with the old sacrifices make the rain come? In the end it was decided that the chief must say no to Kruger: no more land, no more apprentices. He agreed. All the men stood then, holding their spears, and saluted him with deep voices, saying, "Kgabo."

But Paul Kruger and the Boers were angry. They made a plot against Kgamanyane. They would hurt and shame him in front of the tribe. The Bakgatla would see that they were the masters and that the black people were the servants and must do what they were told. They spoke sweet words to Kgamanyane, bidding him come and eat and drink with them at a certain house. His interpreter Mapisa should come, so that all would be made plain.

In this house they had laid out a table with dishes and plates covered with good food, meat, bread, roast fowls,

honey, wine in bottles, and the spirits that make men foolish. Mapisa waited at the door until he was called. Chief
Kgamanyane came in and looked around, but he was uneasy. What was this for?

Suddenly they seized him. There were many of them.
Two got his hands fast with *reims*, two his feet. He saw
that he had been betrayed and he saw one with a *sjambok*,
the heavy, hide whip of the master. Suddenly he dived
under that table of theirs, a heavy table on trestles, and,
bound as he was, he stood upright so that all smashed into
ruin, wine, dishes, bread, meat, all broken around his
bound feet. He knew what they meant to do; it was clear
in their faces. He spoke with the hidden words of a chief;
he said: "Tortoise people fear old dry grass! But why
should I fear old grass when the hail hammers me every
day on the high hill?" And then, as they came near, their
boots splashed with the spilled wine, he shouted at them,
"I may fear the war ax, but when you come to club me
with a *kerrie*, I am not afraid! You can try to break the
tortoise child, but he will go inside his shell!"

And the Boers looked at one another, knowing with
what a man they had to deal, and they dragged him onto
the *stoep* of the house and tied him there. Mapisa had run
to fetch the men of the tribe, but many of them had followed, for they were uneasy when Chief Kgamanyane
went alone to the house of the Boers. More and more
came. And they saw what was being done, but the Boers
made it clear that if they tried to rescue their chief it
would be his death and theirs. He was asked would he
now give the land and the boys to work on it, but he shook
his head. They tied him to a post, tied his hands high so

135

that he could not move. Then they began on him with the *sjambok*. When one was tired, another took it over. They laid his back open. He could not know how many strokes, how long it would go on. He did not know if his people were watching, but he knew he must be as he should be in front of them. No cry must come from him. It is easy to be brave in battle; this was not so easy. Only he cried out in his mind to his father Pilane and to his ancestors, and they told him he had made the right choice. But there would be another choice in front of him. If he lived. For now he was beginning to half die with the pain.

He did not know it was over until he felt them cut the rope above his hands. He fell to the ground and was swallowed up in a blackness, but within it the ancestors said he had done well. Dimly he heard someone laughing, felt a kick land in his stomach. He was half pulled to his feet and then hit in the face. Then he was dropped again. And after a long while, it seemed, his enemies went away, and after that he was being lifted to his feet; it was two of his own counselors, old men, his fathers, and tears were running down their cheeks; he leaned on them and in a while, half carried, he was brought back to his own tribe. And all of them with one voice saluted him as Kgabo, and one leaped out and began to praise him in a quick, tense voice, calling him their father and their child, calling him Bull of Battle, Leader of the Spears. And then water was held to his mouth and he drank.

They were feeling his cuts, exclaiming, weeping, and suddenly his brother Kgari, the rainmaker, was speaking to him, urgently. "Your blood, my brother," he said, "your

136

blood has been accepted by the ancestors. They have spoken to you. Tell us, tell us now what we must do! Raise your head, Kgamanyane!"

And one of his counselors spoke too: "We are your children. Tell us, Kgabo. What you say, that we shall do."

Then Kgamanyane raised his head and every movement was pain. "Men of the Kgatla," he said, "you saw me shamed by my enemies. Tied like a slave. Beaten almost to death. Even though I shut my shell over me. Shamed!"

But one of them said: "We saw. But our chief was not shamed." And all around him others agreed, and murmured praise names.

"This could happen again," said Kgamanyane. "I know. It is only just behind. I feel its breath like a hyena on my heels. It might happen to any one of us. To all of you. There is no battle to be won against these men. Only defeat or death."

Kgari, his brother, spoke: "Did our ancestors say that?"

"I asked them," said Kgamanyane. "Between the strokes of the whip I asked them. So that I should not cry aloud and shame you, men of the Kgatla! And they said—they said: You had a clear choice, Kgamanyane, son of Pilane. You took the road you are on now. We give you another choice. To stay or to go. One way we would be with you."

"And your choice?" asked Kgari, low and tense, and all listened in silence and deep anxiety.

Kgamanyane looked in front of him and now his eyes, which had not wept during the pain, were blurred with tears. "I said I would go. Go from our beautiful land. Go from Moruleng. For Moruleng has become Mmawitlwe,

137

the mother of thorns. And they said, That is the right choice. To go. We shall go with you." He looked painfully around him. "Men of the Kgatla, come with me."

"But where?" they said. "Where is there to go?"

Kgamanyane answered them: "To a drier, thornier place, to harsher lands, where we shall live in peace because they will not want it. We must take our cattle and sheep. We must take our wives and children."

One of the old men spoke: "We have lived here. We have buried. Our wives have given birth. We have been happy in Moruleng. Do we go to nothing?"

Kgamanyane nodded at him and said: "Truly, we go to nothing. And yet we go to a promise. When we helped the Bakwena to get back their cattle from the Bangwaketse, we were promised land whenever we chose to come for it. Now we take up that promise."

There was a murmur of "Kgabo," and the old man spoke: "That is wisdom. But will the Bakwena remember?"

Kgamanyane almost smiled. He said, "We will lengthen their memories if need be. I know also that something will be shown to us by those unseen who go with us. But we must go soon, soon, before they think we have decided, or they will follow with their guns and destroy us and our cattle. I heard them say that they would take our cattle. As a punishment, they said, for disobedience. My disobedience. For which, having punished me, they would punish my people."

And now pain was overcoming Kgamanyane again, and for a while he lay on his face, groaning a little, and Dikolo

138

his Great Wife, and two of his younger wives, Nkomeng and Keiseng, had come running and bathed his wounds with water and laid pads of healing herbs over them. For he was cut from neck to knees, cuts which would not heal into a warrior's scars. But they whispered into his ears that they loved him the more, and Dikolo laid her cheek by his. But the men of the Kgatla were discussing what had been said, anxious, knowing that they must choose now, that they must drive their cattle in. "In three days," said Kgari, "we shall move, and if any man speaks of it to the whites, he dies." And all agreed. The chief had spoken. They went to tell their wives to grind meal and their sons to bring in the cattle.

Kgari sat on the ground beside Kgamanyane, his brother, who had so often been proud and quarrelsome and now lay so low. He knew that soon Kgamanyane would want to speak with him. In a while it came. "Kgari," said Kgamanyane. "Kgari, my brother, listen. They will think we are weakened. As soon as they hear we have left Moruleng, they will chase us, to get our cattle. They must not know where we have gone."

"That will be difficult," said Kgari. "Cattle are easy to trail."

"Kgari," whispered his brother, "I want our footsteps hidden, men and beasts, hidden as though we had walked on air. So that they will not know."

"How?" said Kgari, but his face was set. He understood.

"You can do it," said Kgamanyane. "Only you. I beg you to do it. I have stopped being proud, Kgari. I am only your brother in sore trouble and pain. I want that the hard rain

139

should beat out the tracks of men and women and cattle."

"How can I do this?" said Kgari. "I must sacrifice. A strong sacrifice. You know that." And he thought of what the missionaries had spoken to him about this god who alone did all and who did not ask for sacrifice, only for repentance.

But Kgamanyane, his brother and chief, was still speaking: "I will give you the sacrifice, whatever it may be. Kgari, I am not your elder brother any more. I am your child."

"I do not like to sacrifice," said Kgari. "I do not like to be overwhelmed by the ancestors. To lose myself in the dark while they buzz at me. To become one with them. Why must I do it? Because of your pride? Because you say no to the whites?"

Kgamanyane half raised himself, wincing with pain. "Kgari, my pride left me when I was beaten like a slave. I do not ask for myself, but for my people. Make the sacrifice, Kgari. You can reach backward and forward. Ask the Old Ones to help me now. To help our people."

After a while Kgari repeated it: "To help our people." And then: "I will try."

It was a long trek for the cattle, starting at night, and the women carrying the woven baskets and pots full of meal and whatever could be taken. So many had babies on their backs; they went slowly. And soon Kruger and the Boers were after them, riding hard. It was an easy spoor to follow, west into the country of the Bakwena. Now it seemed as though they would catch up in an hour or two; they had passed a few who had dropped out: the very old, the sick, a woman in labor. Kruger was black angry. One of the others with him pointed at the sky; it looked like a storm ahead, a heavy storm, though it was not the storm season. Then one of them rode over to Kruger and said to him: "Paul, there's something I need to say. You're the one we chose as our leader. We believe in you, Paul. But, burghers, what are we doing? Are we any better than cattle thieves?"

Paul Kruger turned away angrily, his hand on his rifle. "What!" he shouted. "This man, this Kgamanyane, tries to get away from us, his lawful masters, the ones to whom he pays tax. He tries to get away with every beast that would be due to us in tax and fine, and every man and boy that should be ours to work for us!"

But his friend went on: "I can't see it that way, Paul. This Kgamanyane, he was friendly enough once. You got on with him well enough yourself, liked him."

"You can't like them," said Kruger, "any more than you'd like a snake. He's just a rebel. Do you know this, he said to me that I was only elected, and he was born a chief. Setting up to be better than me!"

"He's paid for that, hasn't he?" said the other.

"Not yet," said Kruger. "He's escaping from his punishment."

Suddenly there was a flash of lightning near them. His friend made a last effort: "Paul," he said, "do we want to make him an enemy forever?"

And then the rain began, great drops, and a wind coming nearer and nearer, roaring. Paul Kruger looked in the face of the rain before answering. The Lord had sent the storm: why? Then he snapped out: "Maybe not. The rain's coming. Burghers, turn your horses!"

So Kgari's rain saved the cattle and the Bakgatla themselves. They came a long way and camped on a hill where there were many baboons, a hill called Tshwene-Tshwene. From there they sent messages to Sechele, chief of the Bakwena. At first Chief Sechele wanted them to settle near Molepolole, his capital, but Kgamanyane feared that it might be too near, there would be quarrels over grazing, and indeed the Bakgatla might not be independent. But there was another place, where the Notwani River wound around the flanks of hills, a place that could be fortified if need be. All around was good grazing; there were springs. There were even morula trees to remind them of home. The name of this place was Mochudi. "Let us go there," said Kgamanyane. "I think it will be a good place." So that was agreed and they came to Mochudi to build their houses on the top of a low hill from which one can see every way. Morning or evening, what you see is always beautiful.

This is the story of someone who is, tribally speaking, my great-grandfather, since I myself am one of the Bakgatla of Botswana, my regiment being Matshego. Much of it was told me by my dear friend the tribal historian, Amos Kgamanyane Pilane, himself a grandson of Kgamanyane. When I am at Mochudi, the capital of the Kgatla people, I stay on the top of the hill with the chief, my son Linchwe II, whose great-grandfather, Linchwe I, was born to Dikolo, the Great Wife of Kgamanyane. When I first

142

came, Mochudi was still in the Bechuanaland Protectorate. How the Protectorate came into being will be clear from the story of Khama. From being a Protectorate, it passed peacefully into independence as Botswana.

9 Lobengula of the Amandebele

He stood right across the way, Lobengula, Mzilikazi's son, broad-shouldered, heavy-hipped, eight feet from bare sole to feather tip of headdress: he, Lobengula, in the royal town of Bulawayo, where all was his, the women, the beer and the roasting meat, the young men dancing with their shining spears, the constant sound of rejoicing, the slaves, the people from the north, carrying grain, driving in oxen. The Englishman, Cecil Rhodes, watched in the south in Bechuanaland, wondering how to bribe, trick, or conquer. This was the one chief who stood across Rhodes's dream of a safe and wide white route to the land of gold and for the greatness and glory of the British Empire. Khama of the

Bamangwato watched too. Lobengula had been his enemy, as also his father before him. But was Rhodes a friend? No, and again no.

Lobengula had been installed King of the Amandebele people ten years before, acclaimed by thousands of warriors in regimental plumes and glory, surrounded by the counselors and old friends of his father, Mzilikazi. Soon afterward he wrote to the English Governor of Natal, expressing a wish to dwell in peace and friendship with the whites. He hoped they would not come and trouble his kingdom if he showed that he was not their enemy. But they came. Oh, they came!

It was difficult for Lobengula to know who they were, whether these whites came from Kruger, who it appeared was the ruler of the Transvaal, or from the English, who obeyed a small White Queen who lived far off and sent them guns and all manner of good things, or from the Germans or from the Portuguese. White men all looked alike. All were liars.

Or were they? Robert Moffat, the missionary, had been as a brother to his father, Mzilikazi, and surely he could trust Ujoni, his son John Moffat, as his brother? Ujoni came and was welcomed as always. Whatever behavior he had which was strange and unfitting for one speaking with a king went by without notice taken of it, since Ujoni too was in the power of his strange God, whose mouth he was and of whom he so loved to speak. Lobengula, the Royal Lion, loved Ujoni and was proud to have him as a friend. He did not wish to believe in Ujoni's god, because he knew that his own ancestors would always speak for him before any high and unapproachable god. But the white men had

146

other skills, and he would listen if Ujoni had to speak of this God out of royal courtesy and because Ujoni had greater wonders he could show.

When Ujoni told the Lion Lobengula that if he made two lines on a piece of paper these would go back to the White Queen, who was so royal that all these grown men, her *indunas*, doubtless with many wives and herds of cattle, loved and dreaded her voice, even from far off; and when Ujoni said to him that this was a paper of friendship, Lobengula believed him completely and made the marks. There were those among his counselors who said that this was not wise. They said that no white man could be trusted, but Lobengula thought that he must surely trust the son of his father's friend.

What he did not understand was that Ujoni, the Reverend John Moffat, was also entangled in Rhodes's dream; he too wanted to see a white empire throughout Africa and to overthrow the black kings who ruled by the spear and through bloodshed and fear and sorcery and who would not listen to the words of the Gospel. As he saw it, there would come virtuous and God-fearing white families with little golden-haired children and all would bring good methods of farming and manufacture and honest trade, and the land would be transformed and the Sabbath bells would ring peaceably from village to village. The black men too would live in decent families, all wearing clothes as God intended, and all working industriously under the wise guidance of the civilized whites and sending their children to Sunday School, with no enmity or fear between the Ndebele and the Shona peoples. This was not altogether Rhodes's dream but it was another side

147

of it, and whatever the dream of the whites it meant the ending of the rule of the Ndebele or of any black people, the breaking of the assegai, and the finish of any power or glory or pride.

So when the Lion Lobengula put the marks on the paper, Ujoni did not tell him that what he had signed said not only that there should be perpetual peace between the Queen's people and the Ndebele people but also that Lobengula and his council should make no treaties or sales or sessions of land to any other people without the permission of the English High Commissioner in South Africa. If Lobengula had known that he was putting himself under the authority of this white man, he would not have signed. But he did not know.

Rhodes knew very soon. He was glad. Yet he was so certain that his own view of things was right that he had expected it. He had determined already how he would follow it up. He had his agents, and the amount of money they would need for the necessary bribery meant little to him. Nor did this seem in any way wrong. It was not for his own immediate profit; it was for Queen and Empire, the Flag, the Dream.

Lobengula had expected that now there would be fewer white men coming to Bulawayo asking, demanding, mannerless, going in where it was forbidden, trampling on custom. True, there were now not many Portuguese, Germans, and, above all, Boers. But there were more and more English. Those from the missions constantly said that he or his officers must not do this or that; they became mad at a small killing or an ordinary punishment, without which discipline could not be kept. They need not have

148

looked at such things and yet they did. But others only asked for leave to dig holes in the ground and take out the gold which they so loved. Others again wished to hunt, and especially elephants.

They brought him presents but in return they wanted to eat him up. They were buzzing flies. He would have liked to shake his head like a great, black-maned lion, to roar and see them run. But he must always be careful; if his young men once saw him angry they would spear the lot in one moment, in less time than it takes a tree to fall when the lightning strikes. For the young men, the Majaha, were becoming more and more ready to drink blood. They had been trained strictly as fighters; they had gone through the same discipline as Shaka's young men. It had been pain. What was the use of all that except to fight? Until they had fought, they must not look for wives; they could not touch the delicious flesh of the maidens who danced at the great feast. The smell of meat and maidens which should be bought with blood! The Majaha did not want to stay still. Would the King never give them leave to kill the whites?

But no, no, King Lobengula would not give them that leave. He sent them raiding north to subdue the small tribes that lived in the hills, to bring and drive in the cattle and women, or farther off still to fight the ones who dreamed of the great kingdoms they once had, those who had built the castles, the stone-walled Zimbabwes, on the hills full of ghosts and gold. The Mashona were still powerful magicians, but their spears were not as strong as the spears of King Lobengula's young men.

And many of the older men, the *indunas*, remembered

Mzilikazi and thought it was wrong to stay still and not to conquer. That was the destiny of the Ndebele people, always to conquer, to go on. Yet they too were half afraid of the whites, above all those who were completely sheathed in strange cloth, so that their eyes were almost covered by a great white helmet and even their hands had little leather houses. Many were the councils King Lobengula held. "We cannot trust them," said one *induna* to another. "Let us drive them all out!"

"No," said King Lobengula. "My father the great Bull Elephant trusted Ujoni's father, took him in his arms, let him speak of his god. When I trust Ujoni, I do my father's will."

"But the others—?"

"See what the English did when they gave the whole country that is called the Transvaal to the Boers. The people of that country had trusted them. They had thought they were protected by the English. Not so. They were given to the Boers. They were not even asked or spoken to about this. It was done over their heads."

"The English give us fair words now. But they think we are cattle."

One and another of the councilors spoke, raising his head slowly. The King listened and his stomach was uneasy. Yet another spoke, an old warrior who had fought beside Mzilikazi, leaning forward, his headring glistening in the firelight. "The Boers do not even give us fair words."

"Perhaps it is better to know one's enemies."

"It is in my thought," said Lotse, who was the Chief Counselor, "that we should decide who are the strongest and give them what they want. Then they will keep out the rest."

"What do we get in exchange for this?" the King asked.

"There is talk of guns. The new kind of guns that are called Martini Henri, and food for them. Much food. Gunpowder. Cartridges. And there is talk of a little boat with guns to go on the Zambezi River. And there is talk of money."

"Their kind of money?"

"And that this money should be paid often. And in return they ask to dig these holes in the ground and that no other person should be allowed to dig them."

"The Boers could not come and dig?" the King asked. "The White Queen will send the *impis* to stop them if they come with rifles?"

"The men who ask to dig are the Queen's children. Is she not bound to help them?" said Lotse. And he thought of the money which had been given to him.

"To help them?" said the King, frowning. "But not against us?"

"How? We and they are allies."

"Allies?" said the King slowly, and shook his head. "That is not easy. The young men wish to kill them. What else do young men want? I too was young once. I wish I could let the Majaha go."

But Lotse had earned his money. King Lobengula put his mark on the paper; it was taken back to Rhodes by his agent Rudd, who lost his way in the desert and would have died but for the kindness of the Bushmen, those who were always called the lowest of the low. And slowly it was brought home to King Lobengula what paper this was and how he had handed over all the things under the ground—this ground on which the grass grew for the cattle of the Ndebele nation—and had given to those who wanted to dig in it power to do all they wanted, to get these things out. And that meant little less than giving the entire rights over all his kingdom. And he found out too that Lotse had been bribed and in his anger destroyed him utterly, he and his wives and children and servants, more than three hundred persons. But he never understood how deeply Ujoni had betrayed him, as well as another missionary, the Reverend C. D. Helm, who had advised him to give the concession to Rhodes's group of mining companies, the British South Africa Company.

Then King Lobengula tried all ways to free himself. He began to feel as an elephant feels when there are hunters all around with poisoned arrows. He sent two of his *indunas* to England, who were first stopped at the Cape but later were received by the White Queen. But the letter which the Queen sent to him after they left was taken on the way by Dr. Jameson, the friend of Rhodes, and altered so that it would seem to Lobengula that it was her wish that he should help the company. Perhaps that did not matter very much. Perhaps it would all have been the same in the end. But Lobengula and his people came to think that the white men were utterly without honor and truth and that was what being civilized meant. He did not even get the promised rifles or the little steamer. But what would have been the use? In some way they would have been turned against him. For Rhodes any means was good enough for his end: Lobengula was a dangerous savage; he must go.

Yet the King thought he must somehow make terms, somehow save his people from the hunters. Surely the Amandebele were still worth something? The leaders of the Majaha *impis* could not understand why he would not let them strike. "We would clean every white man out of Bulawayo!" they said. "Our King would never be troubled by them again. Give us the word—we are hungry!"

But Lobengula groaned and answered, "If I give you that word, where one Englishman died a hundred would rise out of the ground to avenge him. Maybe they are even waiting for this; maybe they are hoping for it, the ones who are outside watching, the vultures. My sons, you have learned to fire these rifles a little, but not to make them kill as the white men do. Will you ask me to destroy you?"

And the Majaha complained and told stories of the good days and looked with hate at the white men and almost with hate at their King. He was growing old. He could not run; he lived on beer and praises. How different things had been under the great Mzilikazi! Surely at least they could go out and hunt the tribesmen in the north, make them run and carry off their cattle? The rains had been poor; why should others eat and they not? Surely somehow, somewhere, the name of the Ndebele was still a terror!

But the King looked to the south. If he could have looked to London, he would have seen Rhodes getting his Charter, seeing his dream almost real, with the mining companies financing more conquests for Britain, once he could get rid of Lobengula and his savages. It was quite clear to him that they would have to be destroyed. Jameson his friend came to Bulawayo; he was a doctor and helped Lobengula, who was suffering pain, mostly because he had drunk too often and too much of the white men's drink. He was a cheerful and fearless man too, though his judgment was bad and he was no more honest than any other white man. Yet in a way he liked the Ndebele. And although the promised guns did not come, the money kept on coming, this gold which seemed to mean so much.

It began now to seem more and more certain to King Lobengula that the white men were going to do whatever they chose, that they would dig holes for gold in his land and make roads. They would have their own police and their own courts. They would expect his men to work for them. If they chose to go beyond into Mashona land, he must give them the road. What kind of a king was he now?

He tried to bargain, to change his mind; he tried to frighten them; he tried to tie them down. It was no use. Cecil Rhodes by now had a small army, an *impi*, but with magic-looking lights, moving and brighter than the full moon, and new kinds of guns. Lobengula sent his *indunas* to see and threaten; they came back scared as dogs. It was all too late. Rhodes had won before a shot was fired.

There were words sent to Lobengula from the head *induna* at the Cape, purporting to come from the White Queen to say that all was well, this was not an army but only men come to dig holes for gold. But it did not seem like that to King Lobengula and his council. He called up his army; there was dancing and singing as at the beginning of war. The young men, the Majaha, waited for the word to go. Surely they would get it now! The King told them that if they went they would most certainly all be killed by these new guns. But they did not care. They waited for his word. He did not give it. He himself, the King, was afraid. He wanted to be friends with the whites. Perhaps Ujoni had put it into his head. Truly in a way he wanted it. But the white men did not want to be friends with him.

They wanted war to show the Ndebele once and for all who had the weapons. They got their war in 1893. It was about cattle. What war is not about cattle, or about gold, which buys cattle, or about land, where cattle graze? The Ndebele *impis* met the English not in forest or broken ground, where they would have had some chance, but on an open plain. The *impis* were totally destroyed. "We hit them with everything we had, but hour after hour they kept on coming until they were almost wiped out." Whatever the settlers thought, the white soldiers had nothing but admiration for the black ones.

News came to Lobengula. He felt himself an old man, unable to understand what was happening. Was it that this money, these golden sovereigns which kept coming, were not a payment to him for leave to dig holes in the ground out of which more golden sovereigns would come? Were they in the thought of the whites buying his kingdom? If so, he must send them back quickly, quickly. They were accursed. He put them into bags and tried to get them back to Rhodes—the invisible, always present Rhodes—or to his men. No use. They went astray or were stolen on the way.

Things were going altogether badly: the shaft of the

King's spear splintered and broke; smallpox walked through the kraals; the ancestors would not listen. It was time for the great burning before the enemy came in. The chief entrusted with it was also entrusted with the lives of two white traders who had settled at Bulawayo. They saw the flames overwhelming the King's houses. But he was already far away. Where he went in the end is not clear, nor yet whether he rode away on a great black horse or whether he died of smallpox. And although a grave is shown that some say is a grave of King Lobengula of the Amandebele, maybe it is not his. For surely it is best that no enemy of his or of his people should ever be able to stand over his bones or to say that in the end he was conquered.

That was the end of the Amandebele and the beginning of white rule in Rhodesia. People had been watching all over Africa and especially in Botswana—which was then Bechuanaland. This is where we shall turn next, to someone whose life overlapped Lobengula's and also Kgamanyane's.

There are many books about the beginning of Rhodesia. I suggest one which is partly in the form of a novel: On Trial for My Country, *by Stanlake Samkange (New York: Humanities Press).*

10   Khama of the Bamangwato

There was a chief of the Bamangwato who was fleeing for his life. His name was Ngwato and he was a brave man; he had covered the retreat of his warriors for as long as he could, throwing spear after spear. Now he was wounded and his enemies were after him. He threw himself down breathless, almost ready to die, in a clump of thick bush, pushing in through thorns and binding creepers, lying panting while they hunted him down. Now they were very near. And then, right in front of them, out from the bush where Ngwato was hiding, trotted a *phuti*, a little buck, with its ears spread and eyes wide and watching.

The pursuers saw it and laughed. No use looking in that

patch of bush, anyway! So on they rushed, shouting and beating with their spears, and slowly Ngwato realized that his life had been saved. So the little buck, the *phuti*, became the emblem of the Bamangwato, as you will see if you ever go to the beautiful town of Serowe, nestling under its hills, the capital of the Bamangwato.

That was a long time ago—two centuries ago, at least, before the Bamangwato settled down anywhere; before, even, they were truly a tribe, knowing themselves as such. But Ngwato had children and grandchildren, and so it went, and about the time of Shaka's death, Sekgoma was King of the Bamangwato. A few years later Sekgoma's Head Wife gave birth to a son who was named Khama. He grew up to be a strong boy, a tireless runner—and indeed his name meant the antelope—a gallant hunter, and above all intelligent. It was he who led the warriors of the Bamangwato when Mzilikazi, King of the Amandebele, sent his son Lobengula from his royal town of Bulawayo with a strong regiment, one of the young *impis*, to raid the lands to the west and south and carry off cattle from the peaceable people who would not stand against them. He had reckoned without Khama, who led a force half on foot and half mounted, and attacked the invaders thirty miles from Shoshong. He had some guns at least, and men capable of aiming and firing them. There was a running battle which gave the defenders of Shoshong time to drive back their cattle and pile up stones to fortify the passes leading to the town.

The Ndebele force could not deal with this. Lobengula, on his way back, killed every man, woman, and child of a small clan which had refused to give him guides across the

Kalahari to Shoshong. He took a few of the Mangwato cattle and the young herdboys who had been with them at the cattle posts. But Khama took the southernmost of Mzilikazi's cattle posts in exchange. It is said that once, when the Bamangwato were fleeing from the pursuit of an Ndebele *impi,* Khama stopped, pretending to be hurt; his men, ashamed to desert their chief's son, rallied and came back, and broke the Ndebele charge. Khama had proved himself as a warrior. Even Mzilikazi acknowledged this, saying, "The Bamangwato are dogs, but Khama is a man!"

These were the days when the first white men came up from the south; some came as traders, but others, among them Robert Moffat and his son-in-law David Livingstone, came as missionaries. They tried to speak of their message with King Sekgoma, to tell him of the afterworld and of their god, who had made everything and who might turn his anger onto his children if they disobeyed him. But in order to obey this god, a man must put away all but one of his wives, must not kill or take from another man, must become gentle and obedient and like a child. This was no teaching to lay before a chief, and Sekgoma in Shoshong received the missionaries kindly enough and let them set up a school and teach whoever was inclined to listen, but for himself he had other things to do. Above all, he must fight marauders, and more especially the Ndebele, who constantly harassed him as well as the other Batswana tribes and chiefs, and who had the terrible Zulu weapons and the overwhelming discipline and fierceness of the Zulu war machine. If it was not the Ndebele, it was the Batlokwa, pushed in turn by the Bakololo, for it was a time of terrible wars and a king must be prepared to look

159

after his people. Fortune for him if he had a son who was as good a fighter as Khama! Equally a king must take the fruits of victory, the feasting and drinking, the dancing and killing, the cattle and the women.

But, when for a time he was in exile among the neighboring Bakwena, with a usurper—his half brother, Macheng—wearing the leopard skin of the chief, he let his sons go to a mission school under the charge of the German Lutherans. Khama, the heir, with his much-loved younger brother Kgamane, went to the school, where they learned the white magic, that words could be made visible and pass from one man to another without sound, and even beyond, even from one land or time to somewhere far off and out of reach, and after this they decided that they would follow the rules laid down and finally asked for baptism, together with Khama's wife.

The young man took it with deep seriousness, so much so that he ceased to be willing to help his father with ceremonies and rituals, such as rainmaking. The missionaries, their religion and their ways of life, alone held the key. He had interested his younger half brothers so much that they too began to learn the Christian teaching, and he himself, with Kgamane, for they did all things together, became teachers in a London Missionary Society school. He could not go on with the old beliefs, even though this meant deep offense to his father, whom he loved and feared, even as the Christians loved and feared their father God. But Sekgoma tried Khama too far when he told him that he must take a second wife. Khama refused and then, with a few friends and followers, retreated from the rage of his father into the dry hills and rocks.

160

King Sekgoma, furious with his son, tried the powers of the witch doctors on him, but it was thirst rather than magic which became too much for Khama. There was a reconciliation of a kind. But the next six years were difficult ones. There was constant scheming, during which Macheng came back; then for a time Kgamane, weak when temptation came, wore the leopard skin. King Sechele of the Bakwena was one of the plotters. And yet Khama continued to respect his father, though he hated to see him as he was only too often: drunk from the liquor that the white traders, eager to get concessions out of him or cheat him over a deal, would hand out to the old man.

There came a time when Khama, deeply sad because both his father and Kgamane, the brother whom he loved, had turned against him, went with his followers to Serowe, where there was a spring of good water, and began to build himself a town. He had many with him, and of these a good number were Christian. Serowe was to be a Christian town. But he was attacked again. He trekked farther away yet, but was constantly attacked both by his father and by his brother. He tried to behave in a reasonable way, resisting but not killing, but his opponents were utterly unreasonable. At last his father King Sekgoma died, in 1875, and Khama was installed as chief. The weapons were put into his hands, the leopard skin was laid on his shoulders; the lion skins were put under his feet. The elders adjured him to govern the people lightly, to respect tradition, to be wise and silent. Praises were shouted and songs were sung. The way was open for a new kind of king.

Khama had thought deeply. He had taken certain things

which the white men had brought; the main one was Christianity and whatever seemed to him to go with it. But the white men had brought other things which were not good and the worst of these was brandy. A man might stand up to the beer which was brewed from local grain, but not to this terrible stuff, which the whites used for their own ends. Better indeed to have neither, since, from now on, the people of Africa would have to be very clear-sighted and clearheaded against the dangers they must face. He therefore prohibited both the import of the white man's drink and the brewing of beer. It was a desperately unpopular thing to do, but Khama must have felt himself to be strong enough. God and David Livingstone would have approved, and his own people were tired of civil war. He went on to forbid polygamy and witchcraft, the killing of one of a pair of twins, and certain very cruel forms of punishment. And he also forbade the payment of cattle as *bogadi*, the "bride price," but really the cementing together of two families. *Bogadi* may have gone too far, for some people are always greedy and will spoil anything, but a girl must have felt insulted when no cattle were offered for her. Nor would he countenance the initiation practices which appeared to go against Christian beliefs.

For some time the Bushmen, the Masarwa, had been held as serfs by the stronger and much more developed Batswana tribes. You could ask a man, "And how many Masarwa do you have?" and it would seem right and proper. But Khama began to protect them and see that they had some rights, even though his own family owned more than any other. He also made laws on game protection, so that certain useful species should not be killed off.

He founded a new town with schools and a church at Palapye and smaller villages in many other places. This had a particular convenience when he was anxious to find other outlets for some of his more difficult subjects. And so it went. In fact, he was unendingly busy.

This did not stop him from doing the main business of a chief: hearing cases, sometimes trivial, sometimes very complicated. His mornings would be spent in this: justice was essential if people were to be held together. He would ride out often to the fields, not only his own, but so as to help and advise his people. But often too he had to deal with matters arising from the coming in of whites. Missionaries or teachers would be well received, but most of them were traders or endlessly asking for land and concessions of various kinds, trying to bribe him and then, when that was not possible, going around those who might be induced to plead their cause.

Sometimes they came with a show of force; they had guns and spoke of other guns behind them. In speech with another African, at least certain forms of courtesy were expected; but the whites seldom spoke courteously. It was becoming plain that the Boers, always looking for more and more land, were pressing in from the east. Some of them had settled in the Tati country where gold was to be found—this stuff which drove the whites mad with greed. But many wandered on, with covered wagons and cattle, and the feeling that somewhere there were greener pastures than they had ever seen, somewhere was the Promised Land. The sensible ones asked King Khama's leave before they began to cross from the Crocodile River westward toward wherever they thought they were going. The foolish ones ignored him, answered with threats when he asked by whose leave they had come, refused to take his advice, and often died in the waterless deserts far beyond Serowe.

Whenever he could, he sent them on with advice on water holes or the little rivers that fade out in the long, rainless months of the Botswana summer. Many of them went on into Angola, where they met the Portuguese, who held the same ideas as theirs over the inferiority of the kaffirs, the natural servants and laborers even when there was no longer any international slave trade.

At least Khama was rid of them. But more came constantly, sometimes setting themselves up with flags and boundaries and shooting any trespassers or seizing cattle and holding them at gunpoint. And it was not only the Portuguese in west Africa. Suddenly the Germans came and annexed for themselves a huge country: South-West Africa. It was of course full of people, but that made no difference to the Europeans. They simply took what they wanted and the people must learn who their new masters were. In fact, the British had assumed power over Bechuanaland in 1885, but it had made very little practical difference.

Khama and the other chiefs were becoming more and more anxious. What would be the future for them? Was there any way of protecting themselves? They tried to find out what was happening elsewhere. Was there any place in Africa where the Africans were safe? It seemed to them that the lesser evil was the British government, represented not by settlers, who were little if at all better than the Boers, but by the government officials and the army

164

officers, who got rid of the marauding Boer trekkers and miners and who spoke in words they could understand.

The wise Moshesh had put himself under the protection of the White Queen. Since then he had been scarcely interfered with; the Boers had kept their distance. Would that be the best thing to do? Chief Khama talked this over with his fellow chiefs, Sebele of the Bakwena and Bathoen of the Bangwaketse, representing the biggest and most solidly established tribes. Things were getting dangerous, because, in the Cape Parliament, Cecil Rhodes was demanding the annexation of Bechuanaland. Rhodes was already dealing with Lobengula. The end was in sight.

Khama had no reason to be friendly with the Ndebele, who had so often raided his lands, and at one point he sent two of his regiments to help the British forces. He withdrew them as soon as it was apparent that the objective was won; there was no point in their following up among the smallpox-ridden kraals of the dying Ndebele. He and his men were congratulated, but he must have watched very carefully to see what would happen next. Suppose the white men became too powerful? If Rhodes got what he wanted, the whole country would pass from the easy, official rule of the far-off British government to the immediately profit-seeking British South Africa Company. It would mean prospectors and traders coming in freely, setting up liquor shops, taking what land they liked, and treating Khama's subjects as though they belonged to them. They would make trouble, taking the side of younger brothers or cousins in the endless power disputes within the tribe, making sure that they at least gained by it, and they would insist on holding their own courts, so that the administering of justice would be taken out of the hands of the chiefs. It did not seem to the Batswana that the conquered people of Rhodesia, the Mashona and the Ndebele, were happy or prosperous. Khama consulted his missionary friends and decided that he and the other two chiefs must go to England. He put it quite simply: "There is no government we can trust as we can trust that of the great Queen. We pray you, therefore, not to throw us away as if we were troublesome children."

For very many British officials that was exactly what they were. How much simpler if Rhodes would take Khama and his like off their hands! In fact, Rhodes met Khama and the others and doubtless tried to find out what exactly they were up to and what further persuasions could be used. Doubtless too he laid on a lavish entertainment, but it is possible that it was not appreciated. This was someone very different from Lobengula, this tall, dignified elderly man who could practice a gentle evasion in which plain statements were made to vanish. And underneath there was something very tough.

It must have taken all Khama's courage to undertake the journey to England, after leaving his son Sekgoma in charge at Palapye, which was his main capital. He must have known that Sekgoma was not the kind of young man who would follow his patterns of rule, nor did it make things easier that his son-in-law Ratshosa, who was also his secretary and general assistant, should have been left behind too. A difficult situation was bound to develop. Perhaps he thought that responsibility might bring more maturity to Sekgoma, favorite child of his first wife, who had died many years back. Perhaps he simply felt that what he had to do in England was more important than anything else.

In the days of the greatest spread of the British Empire and the enormous profits which were coming in from it, the Colonial Secretary was one of the most important people in the government. Joseph Chamberlain was in great sympathy with Rhodes, with the idea of the all-red route, the railway from Cape to Cairo, all under the flag which Chamberlain so genuinely revered. He advised the chiefs to make the best terms they could with the company, and then went off on holiday.

The chiefs, however, stayed. They had determined to go higher, and they had an increasing amount of vaguely anti-imperialist, liberal feeling on their side. Strings were pulled. The two missionaries who were with them had considerable contacts. They were taken to see the sights of London, were asked to country houses—a half-familiar atmosphere of horses and dogs—Khama too had his petted hounds. The invitation to Windsor Castle duly came. They were received by Queen Victoria, who appeared to be genuinely taken with them and pleased with their gifts of leopard-skin karosses—the royal symbol, which they had all themselves worn on their shoulders. She gave them Bibles in the Kuruman translation by Moffat, but each rebound with the royal coat of arms in gold on the cover, the familiar lion and less familiar unicorn. In Khama's copy was written: "The secret of Khama's greatness." She also gave them framed photographs of herself, a color slide, and one of her favorite Indian embroidered shawls for wife or daughter. Now they knew she was real, though so small, and living in the midst of this enormous house filled with soldiers in scarlet and silver. But, best of all, the Queen had been sufficiently interested to change Joseph Chamberlain's mind.

When he came back from his holiday, he found that the chiefs had been talked to by some of the chief men in the South Africa Company and had not liked it. Perhaps there had been too much plain speaking; perhaps the company had underestimated the intelligence of the Africans, who saw quite clearly that the company wanted "to take our land and sell it so that they may see gain." They also realized that "the company wants to impoverish us so that hunger may drive us to become the white man's servants and dig in his mines and gather his wealth." They could not have put it more accurately, and, in order to avoid this, they were willing to give up some of their land.

So it was arranged. The chiefs gave up some of their land, notably the Tati Concession, the Tuli Block, and a strip for the railway, which also cut across the lands of other tribes, including the Bakgatla. But these tribes had been turned over to the South Africa Company, so that there was nothing to be done about it at the time. Fortunately for them, the Jameson Raid put the company in such a bad light with the British authorities that the other tribes were taken out of its jurisdiction and became part of the Protectorate. But this was a historical accident. Meanwhile, the railway was thrust through.

But the main thing had gone King Khama's way. He came back in triumph, but alas only to find that his son Sekgoma had not ruled as his father would have liked: he had not made himself respected by the elders but had encouraged the young men in new notions and ways of doing things. He had also become heavily entangled in the family feuds which had been going on for some time. Perhaps Khama was too harsh; he ended by sending his son into exile. The patience and generosity which he gave in full measure to so many people, white or African, was not shown to his son. Did he expect too much? Did he listen too readily to Ratshosa? Did he not see that the young must be ridden on a loose rein?

Khama of the Bamangwato had been married three times. Two of his wives had died; one had been divorced. Apart from Sekgoma, he only had daughters. He married again when he was well over sixty, a young woman of good family, a Christian and educated; her name was Semane, the Honeycomb. And at last they had a son. They called him Tsehekedi. He was born at Serowe, since the capital at Palapye was beginning to be short of water. Khama built a great dam between the Swaneng Hills. After his time it went to ruins, but now it has been rebuilt by the boys of Swaneng Hill School and behind it there is a great sheet of water all the year long, and behind that again, fields of crops, as Khama would have wished.

But there was a sad aftermath of the Protectorate treaty. Khama had agreed to move the Mabirwa, a small tribe, from the far side of the railway whenever the settlers in the Tati Block, which he had ceded, were in need of the land. For many years nothing happened. But the Tati Block had been ceded to the South Africa Company, partly for mining, partly for ranching, and suddenly the company complained to the Bechuanaland Protectorate

Administration that the Mabirwa were good-for-nothing poachers and must go. The Administration reminded Khama of his promise, now a quarter of a century back, to move the Mabirwa as and when necessary. The time had come.

Khama gave the job of moving the Mabirwa out to one of his headmen, Modisa-o-Tsile, who happened also to be his son-in-law. It was carried out with a large force of soldiers provided by Khama and with complete ruthlessness. Modisa-o-Tsile and his men treated the Mabirwa as enemies, and killed and tortured and looted, just as their fancy took them. Those who had been captured were tied up and marched to the *kgotla* of Modisa-o-Tsile and for all practical purposes enslaved. The chief of the Mabirwa was no doubt a difficult man; he did various things which had angered Khama. But he had been brutally treated. It was sad that Khama's old age should have been stained with this injustice. But sadder still, perhaps, that it ended in a mist of quarrels among members of his own family, with too many people looking for power, which had been too much concentrated. At least there was a reconciliation between father and elder son Sekgoma before the end. And there was a baby son born to Sekgoma: Seretse. But the baby's grandfather could never have foreseen Seretse's life or his future presidency of Botswana, the old Protectorate, now independent.

Khama was ninety or near it when he rode out one day to his cattle post, drove in a herd of cattle through dust and choking heat, then through a thunderous downpour. He went home, caught a chill, died. The clear spring had dried. The rock was split. People had to think again.

If Khama III had not had the courage and determination to go to England and insist on a protectorate at the time he did, it is most unlikely that the Bechuanaland Protectorate would have come into being. Nor would there have been much chance for it to become an independent country as Botswana in 1966, with Khama's grandson, Sir Seretse Khama, as President, and with a good chance of the kind of peaceful development which all of us want. Khama is buried at Serowe, with a bronze statue of a buck, the emblem of the Bamangwato, over his grave.

11 The Great Tree Falls

Here was the young prince, brought up for courage and
endurance and for military skill, listening carefully to the
stories of his forebears and his nation, watching his head-
ringed elders in council or at their leisure, alert for behavior in matters of conduct or in the code of manners, thinking over matters of justice and knowing that the time
might come when he himself, Cetshwayo, would be the
supreme judge of the Zulu nation. The supreme commander too, if things fell out as he and his friends wanted.
But his father would not say. And there were other claim-
ants, especially his half brother, Mbuyazi.

Yet had not he, as a boy, weapon and food bearer to his

173

father, seen red war in the days of Dingaan his uncle? But his father, Mpande, King of the Zulus, had not cared for the wetting of the spears. He loved things of peace, the warm, scented huts of his wives, the dances of his warriors. But how should a warrior dance, in mock battle, with all the plumes and panoply of a fighter, and then be denied the real thing? King Mpande never led his armies to war; he was afraid of whites, the men with the guns and horses. Better to keep on the right side of them, especially of the Boer farmers, who were forever raiding cattle and carrying off boys and girls into slavery. The British? Well, they were farther off, and on the whole they were not farmers but soldiers; he could understand them.

Meanwhile, one could have a small war with the Swazis. He would send an army. Young Cetshwayo and his regiment, the Tulwana, with their white shields and splendid headdresses, acquitted themselves well. The Swazis ran, losing many men and much cattle. Among the Zulus there was much talk of Prince Cetshwayo. Was he to be the leader they were looking for?

Dangerous for Mpande to have these young cockerels crowing so loud! He set Cetshwayo and Mbuyazi at one another's ears. There was a horrible and bloody battle in which brother killed brother, and women and children were pushed screaming down the slopes into the flooded Tugela, into the jaws of the flapping, crunching crocodiles. It was clear that, whatever his father may have wished, Cetshwayo would now be the King of the Zulu nation.

But the evil genius of Zululand had come into his life; this was the English adventurer, Dunn, who made his way into the confidence, first of King Mpande, then of Cetshwayo. The Africans still had a lot to learn about the character and motives of white people, and were easily taken in by a good presence, a horse, a rifle, and promises of being on their side. A few "Tower" muskets, sold to Cetshwayo at an inordinate profit, also brought Dunn a large grant of land, and with it power equivalent to that of a chief. Here was a storybook situation, with the white hero lording it over the savages; that was how Dunn might have put it to himself. In real life it was different. The Zulu people did better in putting their trust in Theophilus Shepstone, the Secretary for Native Affairs in Natal, whom they called Somsteu. He was fully as brave a man as Dunn, though less showy, and he attempted, anyhow at first, to behave with real honesty.

There was constant encroachment from the Boers. They would see a bit of land with nobody at the moment in occupation; it was too much of a temptation for men who were pathologically land-hungry and seemed never to be happy unless settled so far from one another that they could not see their neighbor's smoke but could feel themselves absolute monarchs. When the Zulus complained about this to the British authorities, they temporized, very unwilling to quarrel with their prickly neighbors, who had walked out of Natal because they could not stand British rule and had formed themselves into the Transvaal Republic with strong military leaders and a Volksraad much like the Zulu Council. Finally, the Zulus begged the Natal government to set up a strip of land between them and the Boers, to be governed by Natal, with whom they had never had any boundary disputes. The Governor of Natal was willing, but the President of the Transvaal Republic less so; matters were dragged out and nothing was done. The main disputed territory was a very large area, perhaps an eighth of the already diminished Zululand, said to have been promised to the Boers by Mpande, though this was always denied by his counselors and his family.

Then King Mpande of the Zulus died and the grim burial rites took place; for his servants and wives must go with him. Cetshwayo had been duly chosen as the heir and now the Zulu nation sent to Natal to ask Somsteu to prepare himself "to arrange the family of the King." In time the British authorities arranged a fine military escort for Somsteu, including two field guns. As they had taken some months to make these arrangements, part of the coronation had already taken place. No king can keep fifteen thousand hungry warriors quiet for months!

The doctoring of the new King and the giving of magic protection took place in the great kraal, as did the ceremony of starting the new fire for the new reign. After this he was led out, in his new greatness, to the graves of the ancestors, who would now watch over him, alerted by the sacrifice of black oxen. Then, back at the great kraal, Masipula the Chief Councilor gave into his hand the spear of the Zulu kings, the spear of sharp war, of quick justice and punishment of rebels. All shouted the royal salute: Bayete. Only, there were two or three powerful chiefs who did not entirely join in, especially one called Zibebu.

After this there was feasting and many of the warriors left. Shepstone, at last arriving, felt that he had been slighted and sent a sharp note to the young King, who in return sent apologies and gifts, including valuable ivory.

176

Arrangements were now made, in the course of which Cetshwayo told Shepstone about his continuing difficulties with the Boers. It seems that Shepstone thought highly of his ability and grasp of a situation, but was naturally anxious as to what kind of king he would make. Fireworks were provided, and a marquee for the presents, as well as a chair of state and a crown adapted from Zulu ideas by the master tailor of the 75th Regiment. The Natal Volunteers had their rifles and revolvers loaded with live ammunition; there was a certain absence of trust. But nothing untoward happened, except that, while the Volunteers were sightseeing, some of their horses bolted among the spectators.

Shepstone had insisted on a set of new laws, designed to limit bloodshed and killing without trial or a right of appeal. He did not think these would make an immediate difference, but perhaps they might in time. In many ways Somsteu admired the Zulus, but also wanted to change them. After all, he had been asked to be Father to the nation.

When the talk was finished, Somsteu put the mantle and crown onto Cetshwayo and all ended happily. But there was still much to be discussed, including the position of missionaries, a difficult question, and above all relations with neighboring countries. More presents were exchanged and the British party returned, leaving Zululand to settle down under its new King.

But how to be King, how to wield the spear, when all was forbidden? The young fighters were impatient; the older ones, who had perhaps been in the terrible last battle with Dingaan, the slaughter at Blood River, smiled and mocked at them. Cetshwayo himself tried to look all ways; but above all he must conciliate and yet show himself to be strong with the *indunas,* the great commanders, who alone had power, if they chose, to rise against the King. They watched him, as he them. He insisted on all his genuine rights, for instance the collecting and checking of the royal herds of cattle. But there was another right and also duty of a new Zulu King. He must lead his warriors out to wash their spears in the blood of an enemy.

The Swazis? But there were many white people who had made their way into Swaziland and started farming there. It was good land. These whites might be involved. Somsteu forbade this war. Dunn acted as go-between and Cetshwayo trusted him. But again and again the Boers from the Transvaal came over the border, casually shot innocent people and carried off cattle, finally, under President Joubert, annexing a huge area about which they had earlier agreed to arbitrate. The official complaints of the Zulu Council had no success. Cetshwayo's own letter foreshadows a still grimmer year: "I cannot," he said, "submit to being turned out of my own house. It may be that I will be vanquished but, as I am not the aggressor, death will not be so hard to meet."

Yet the Transvaal Republic was having its own difficulties. Sekukuni of the Bapedi had fought back, unexpectedly, when they attempted to take over his territory. News of that war came through quickly into Zululand. If the Bapedi can fight, so all the more can we! The Griquas killed; there was killing away in the lands of the Baherero; guns do not always win. We are ready now. Must we always do what the English want? Somsteu is away. He has forgotten us. The Boers go on coming into our lands. Let us teach them a lesson. Let it be their blood which our spears drink!

Cetshwayo tried to calm down the *indunas,* but he too was angry and frustrated. He hit back at a regiment of girls, the Ingcugce, who refused to marry the men from a senior regiment which had just been given permission to marry. For the old discipline of Shaka's time was still kept up and men might have to go for many years unmarried. This was surely a mistake in these days when Zululand could no longer be an expanding military empire. If Cetshwayo had really wanted peace, he would have let people settle down earlier to married life and interests. They would have been less restless and the smoldering anger between his special followers, the Usutu, and those who had supported his brothers and now supported Zibebu might have died down. Yet it would have been a break with a proud tradition and the *indunas* might well not have agreed. Nor might Dunn. Zululand at war did not suit him, but neither would a peaceful and united country have given him the same chances of profitable deals with both sides.

As it was, the girls refused to marry these middle-aged men; some already had young lovers in junior regiments. Some ran away. Several—perhaps seven—were killed and their bodies laid out at the crossroads as a warning to the nation against disobedience. Nor were their parents, on pain of death, allowed to bury them. This was not to be the end of the affair; what is certain is that Shaka would have acted with far more severity.

Another Shepstone, brother of Somsteu, was now Secre-

179

tary for Native Affairs in Natal; he heard, expressed deep concern, and sent messages demanding an explanation. Cetshwayo and his Council felt that they were being interfered with by outsiders who did not understand what keeping order in Zululand entailed. "My people will not listen unless they are killed," said King Cetshwayo, and again: "Do I go to Natal and speak to the Governor about *his* laws?" He wanted to be friends with the English, but he was not going to be overruled by them. The *indunas* agreed. They too were in a killing mood. Mobilization of the regiments began.

But things were going on over their heads. Back in England, in 1876, it had been decided, largely by Lord Carnarvon, Secretary of State for the Colonies, that South Africa must be united on a large scale, no longer just government from the Cape with independence for the Transvaal or any other state these unmannerly Boers chose to set up, and Natal virtually self-governing, but a great imperial domain. By now it was quite clear that there were considerable mineral riches in this uncomfortable land; large diamonds had been found. The City of London was concerned. In India the Viceroy was more gorgeous and impressive than all the Rajas: it must be the same in Africa. Sir Bartle Frere, with much Indian experience, was to go out as High Commissioner for Southern Africa and Governor of the Cape, while Sir Garnet Wolseley was to dispense lavish hospitality in Natal. Theophilus Shepstone, now knighted, was to deal with the Transvaal Boers, who after their defeat by Sekukuni, appeared to be more willing for British protection. All looked easy from London: the Boers would be civilized; the blacks, duly protected, would know their places; the gold and diamonds would flow into the proper channels.

But by the time Sir Theophilus arrived at the Cape—and a ship might take more than a month from Southampton—the Transvaalers had thought better of it. Sekukuni had not followed up his victory. All he wanted was to get rid of trespassers on his land; he had not got around to "civilized" ideas of total defeat of one's adversary. However, the Boers of the Transvaal had largely defeated themselves by being so devoted to personal freedom, as they had shown by walking out from the Cape, that they were now refusing to pay any taxes. Government could not be carried on without money.

What was Shepstone to do? Cetshwayo with fifty thousand men was waiting for the moment to strike the Boers in the Transvaal. Should that be allowed to happen? If it did, both sides would be desperately weakened and England could step in, pick up the bits, and incorporate them in Carnarvon's design. But Shepstone, and Sir Bartle Frere above him, could not agree to this. It would have meant the impossible thing, to allow a war in which blacks might win a victory over whites. Somsteu said no.

It was a terrible disappointment for King Cetshwayo and his *indunas*. His Father, Somsteu, had betrayed him. How was he to send back his young men? They might think there was never going to be any war. They might rise against him and demand their rights as warriors. And it would have been so easy for Somsteu to look the other way for a short time!

The main boundary quarrel, the disputed territory, was now going to arbitration; but the King had other troubles.

It was the Ingcugce girls again, and a fight between two regiments, lovers and husbands, which started with sticks but went on to spears. Some of the men were killed, but the whole affair was blown up quite out of proportion by Sir Bartle Frere. It was to be the first step in a series of diplomatic exaggerations, designed to make the imperialist policy acceptable in England. It was essential to make out that the Zulus were a crowd of blood-stained savages who could only understand strong measures. Sir Henry Bulwer, the Governor of Natal, did not entirely share these views; what interested him was not crushing the Zulus but keeping peace. He thought that arbitration by the Boundary Commission, if honestly carried out, would have that effect: "If the Zulus are in earnest to have it settled peaceably, we certainly must be very much in earnest with the same object."

And what was Somsteu doing? He had gone over to Pretoria, interviewed President Burgers and Vice President Paul Kruger, and found the country in a state of considerable difficulty, with no money to pay for anything, even though the intelligent realized the diamond potential. But what were future diamonds to farmers determined to go on living the kind of life they wanted? After welcome presents of sherry and champagne but less welcome discussions, Somsteu ran up the British flag and formally annexed the Transvaal.

Meanwhile, the Boundary Commission sat, duly discounted various forged documents, and came out flatly that there had been "no cession of land at all by the Zulu King, past or present, or by the Zulu nation." Had Cetshwayo been told this, he would have been happy and, once it had been made public and acted upon, the Zulus would have settled back, feeling that justice had been done. But for nearly six months Sir Bartle Frere sat on it and no word was allowed to go through to the anxious Zulu King and his people. It seems only too plain that this was deliberately done in the hope that the Zulus might be provoked into some action which would provide the excuse for crushing them and carrying out Carnarvon's policy.

Unhappily, some action did take place which could be used for anti-Zulu propaganda—Carnarvon was no longer the Colonial Secretary, but his policies continued, approved by Disraeli and the aging Queen Victoria. Two unfaithful wives, daughters-in-law of Chief Sirayo, fleeing from the wrath of their husbands, were chased into Natal, brought back, and put to death, as Zulu law demanded. The King did not even know what had happened, but he was told to arrest the husbands and send them into Natal for trial and punishment. He explained that he could not do this: they were his subjects and the whole matter must be discussed at the Great Council; he offered compensation, plenty, it was thought, for two women, but it was not enough. And again, two quite harmless British subjects were suspected of being spies and were detained and frightened. Once more, it was an accident and nothing to do with King Cetshwayo, but Sir Bartle Frere blew it up into "a most serious insult and outrage."

A further incident involved an attack on some Swazi kraals, with killing and robbery. This was no doing, even, of the Zulus; the leader was an ex-Swazi, a brigand, who was in fact outlawed by Cetshwayo. But this was not how

Sir Bartle Frere saw it. He felt that the time was now ripe for his ultimatum to Cetshwayo. Public opinion had been worked up in England. The Zulus were out of hand, insolent, unconquered. Yes, unconquered, that was it. Time for the Mother of the Free:

Wider yet and wider, may thy bounds be set.
God, who made thee mighty, make thee mightier yet.

This must, in all sincerity, have been what echoed in the hearts of Sir Bartle and many another. He did not allow any actual facts to come between him and his noble vision.

Meanwhile, Cetshwayo was organizing hunts to keep his young soldiers busy and was waiting anxiously for the result of the Boundary Commission. Why had his English friends deserted him? John Dunn doubtless reassured him. In fact, the Colonial Secretary had written to Sir Bartle Frere, urging the importance of making the result known to Cetshwayo. But this had no effect. When he published it, he put out at the same time and without even consulting Sir Henry Bulwer, the Governor of Natal, a memorandum which in effect undid the award. Yes, it was agreed that the land belonged to the Zulus, but they would have no power to turn out the Boer farmers, who, earlier on, had had the land allocated to them by their own government; they would now be able to occupy it safely under British guarantee. This might help with the hard feelings left by Shepstone's annexation of the Transvaal.

It was now merely a question of how and when to tell King Cetshwayo that a very large slice of his country was to be colonized by the men he hated most, who would then be protected by British arms. Meanwhile, Sir Bartle Frere put every pressure onto the Colonial Secretary in London to send more troops, so that the outcome of war could be certain. He was much helped by the voices of the traders and of the missionaries, many of whom had been found to be completely subversive of the Zulu moral order. For this had happened only too often. Everything which had kept people together, every custom and loyalty and obedience, had been attacked by the missionaries; many converts simply did anything they liked, so long as it was against established law and custom and so long as they stayed within the protection of the missions. Military service and polygamy were alike banned. A man who was unwilling to take his part in the defense of his country and who was willing to throw out a loyal wife who had worked for him and borne him sons—what kind of man was that? If the missions wanted to fill Zululand with such people, they could not be tolerated. Many of them had been told to go, and they lost no time in rousing Church opinion against the tyrant Cetshwayo.

But he had one friend in the Church and he knew it. This was Colenso, Bishop of Natal, whom the Zulu called Sobantu, and with him Frances his wife, who was "not partial to savages of any color" but hated injustice, and especially his daughter Harriette, whom Cetshwayo thought of, and rightly, as his sister. It is through Frances Colenso's letters that we see the other side of the mirror, Somsteu gradually becoming more official and ambitious, less concerned with Africans as people, while his brother was completely one with Natal opinion.

How did it look to Cetshwayo when, in December 1878,

fourteen of his chiefs, with John Dunn, whom he still trusted, went to a meeting on the Natal side of the Tugela River? First, the award of the commission was read, giving the disputed territory to the Zulus. It was not yet broken to them that the land would be taken up by Boer colonists, with a British Resident to see that they were not interfered with. However, immediately following the award, an ultimatum was read and translated to the Zulus. It said that Chief Sirayo's sons, and others responsible for the capture of the runaway wives, were to be handed to the whites, doubtless to be hanged for murder, in addition to a fine of five hundred cattle. Another hundred cattle were to be paid for the insult to the two whites. And before the end of twenty days.

But after this came a long statement of what must be done so that the King of the Zulus "will have contented subjects." This included the total disbandment of the regiments and the end of the military system, with leave for every young man to marry at his pleasure; it also included the appointment of a British officer, a Deputy High Commissioner, to see that everything was carried out. All this to be done within thirty days, "for the safety and welfare of the Zulu people."

The welfare of the Zulu people? One of the King's counselors asked, "Have the Zulus complained?" But of course that had never been a genuine consideration. If it had been, Cetshwayo and the Great Council could have been approached about a gradual change from a military state to something more settled, with alternatives and inducements. They might well have listened, especially if Somsteu had come back to them, or Sobantu. But force was quicker and simpler. There was some attempt at arguing about the terms, but Shepstone, Somsteu's brother, would have none of it. They must go straight back and tell the King.

Twenty days for one ultimatum, thirty days for the other! And the rivers in flood. Loyal subjects to be given up as well as all those cattle. Surely they would at least give him time to consult with his Council at due length? No, rigid punctuality was the rule. It was the same rule of punctuality which had been the downfall of MacDonald of Glencoe, hampered by snow from taking his oath in time and so giving his enemies the excuse for the massacre.

Cetshwayo tried at least to collect the cattle, feeling all the time that some bargain must be possible. But Sirayo's friends and clan meanwhile refused to give up his sons or even to let the cattle of the fine leave the country. The regiments, scattered about the country, refused to be disbanded. What next?

Cetshwayo knew the strength of the British army, which would now be used against him. He knew what they could do to him. He had heard how they had dealt with Kreli the great Chief of the Xhosas, what had happened to Gaikas and Pondos. Only Moshesh of the Mountain of the Night had managed to keep his country, though now it was under the protection of the English, and he was dead, his son Letsie ruling Lesotho in his stead: for how long? Nobody knew. Only in the north was it possible to hold out against the whites. Mzilikazi was dead, but his son Lobengula was still strong. And he himself, Shaka's heir, what chance had he? It may be that he called on

Shaka, his uncle, to look on him favorably; it may be that Shaka came to him in dreams. But had Shaka ever had to face the great English guns, which were pulled by teams of horses and which could shatter a stone fort or kill twenty men at once? Oh yes, Cetshwayo was warned. Perhaps if he stayed within the boundaries of Zululand they might not attack him there. Or perhaps something would happen to stop disaster.

But the young men who were now called up in their regiments to fight in defense of their country, they had no anxieties. They were duly doctored. They were not afraid. They were going to win.

But John Dunn had ridden to the Tugela. He wanted to remain neutral, but this was impossible. Lord Chelmsford, who had been given command of the army, answered heartily that he must make his choice; he must come over to their side of the river with as many men as he could get. They would look after him. Dunn decided he would fight on Chelmsford's side against the King, who had trusted and befriended him.

Lord Chelmsford was not a man to take advice; he felt it was all going to be very easy. He paid no attention to local warnings. He did not understand that the Dutch, including Vice President Kruger, were in earnest and knew just what sort of opponents he was up against when they told him he must always be sure to *laager* his wagons every evening and always when the enemy was near. But that was not something which made sense to Chelmsford's cavalry officers. He decided to attack across the Tugela and over country which was particularly difficult owing to the rains. But perhaps he thought the Zulus, tired of the tyranny and oppression of Cetshwayo, would surrender when they saw the British guns. Whether they did or not, this savage must be made to fight, so as to get the real punishment he so richly deserved.

And so to the battle of Isandhlwana.

It was a complete defeat for the British. In spite of some differences of opinion among the *indunas,* the Zulu plan of campaign was successful far beyond their own hope. The Commander in Chief, Mnyamisna, and his general Tshingiswayo had an excellent scout service; they knew every movement of Chelmsford's columns before Chelmsford himself did. Cetshwayo and Tshingiswayo had both come to the conclusion that if an instant victory could be gained it would be possible to come to terms and emerge with honor. After some early skirmishing, the battle started with the Umcityu regiment rushing in to the attack with their black shields and red headdresses. Then all attacked in the classical chest and horns movement and with the perfect Zulu discipline and courage. But who would have thought they could have taken first a rocket battery and then the field guns, finally the whole camp? When it came to infighting, an assegai was more deadly than a revolver. The battlefield was choked with bodies.

Even Chelmsford had to realize what had happened and started withdrawing. But a few of the British under two junior officers, and a number of hospital patients, were cut off at the Swedish mission station at Rorke's Drift, just on the Natal side of the Tugela. They were attacked by the best soldiers of the Zulu army, part of the Undi army corps, including the King's own regiment, the Tulwana. They had been told to cut off the retreat of the whites after Isandhlwana, but the British soldiers who managed to escape took a shorter road and so got away. The Undi men, angry at having had no chance to fight, pressed their general, Dabulamanzi, one of the King's brothers, to let them attack the Rorke's Drift station.

This was against orders. Cetshwayo had forbidden his army to attack fortified positions, but this *impi* was the kind who would pull bayonets out of rifle sockets with their bare hands. In the end, the little garrison was relieved by reinforcements from Chelmsford. Another body of English troops was bottled up in Eshowe for more than two months. If they had not taken the kind of defensive measures that Chelmsford had been too grand to take, they would have been slaughtered. Now all the forces were halted, waiting for reinforcements from England. They were bound to come, even though Sir Henry Bulwer in Natal and the Colonial Secretary in London both disapproved profoundly of Frere's ultimatum and the ensuing war. But it would be unthinkable, especially with the Transvaalers saying what they were saying, to let a British force admit defeat by a bunch of black, heathen savages! So when King Cetshwayo sent messages asking for negotiations with a view to peace, Chelmsford refused to consider them.

At this time it would have been easy for Cetshwayo to invade Natal and do immense damage. Some of his generals urged him to do this, but he gave the strictest orders that they were not to attack Natal, though they must be ready to die in defense of Zululand. "The English are attacking me in my own country," the King said, "and I will defend myself in my country. I will not send my *impis* to kill them in Natal, because I and those who went before me have always been good friends with the English." But their good friends were little help to the Zulus now. Three months after Isandhlwana, Colenso wanted to go and bury the dead, or at least their white bones. He knew he would be safe with Cetshwayo. But the Natal authorities would not allow it. It would be "a step toward peace"! Frances Colenso writes: "It does seem hard that the ear of our government should be inexorably closed to any overtures from C. It is they seemingly who thirst for blood."

The reinforcements arrived. But first there had been other minor defeats for the British to bear, including the disaster of Hlobane. But Chelmsford's officers were learning. At Kambula, the Ngobamakosi, one of the finest regiments, charged again and again, with utter disregard for their losses. The British were beaten back at first, but after a while their superior firing power asserted itself. The Zulus had inferior rifles or muskets, and insufficient training with them. Almost 2,000 Zulus lay dead for the loss of little more than a score of English. The King and his generals had been building up the army, but now men began drifting back to their kraals, trying to protect their cattle from British raiding parties and hoping the storm would blow over. Cetshwayo was angry and desperately uneasy, for now the garrison at Eshowe was relieved and all was set for a new attack with the reinforcements from England.

News of what was happening must have come in to the King almost continually. When his peace offers were rejected, he knew what the end was bound to be, yet never imagined it could be as bad as it was. Some at least of his senior *indunas* and counselors must have known, and probably Mnyamisna, his Chief Counselor. But others were determined to fight. Under the old order, it was toward this that all their lives had pointed. If their King, their war leader, the inspired of Shaka, told them not to fight, that was a nonsense, something not to be believed. They would fight and their generals must lead them.

Meanwhile, Chelmsford's columns came in, with far more artillery and engineers. They moved slowly and Chelmsford heard to his great annoyance that he had been superseded by Sir Garnet Wolseley. But he refused to halt; he was determined to be revenged on Cetshwayo. The armies had moved some way into Zululand when three envoys arrived to discuss peace terms. Now the conditions were hard: all arms, including the captured field guns, to be collected and given up; cattle of course; and a named Zulu regiment to come and lay down its arms before the British camp. They went back to the King and told him. He did not like the terms but was prepared to accept them. But it had to be discussed, especially the matter of the regiment. He was no despot who could simply give orders to his subjects. And there was something else. A sickness was striking his cattle—not only his, but all the cattle in Zululand. It was as though the gods and the ancestors had turned their backs on him.

Meanwhile, the white army advanced, slowly, at the

pace of the ox wagons. For these men could not be sepa-
rated from their bedding and food; they must eat, not porridge, but bread; they must have hot tea to drink. But they
were as dangerous as a forest fire. They swept up every
cow or ox they could see. They burned every kraal. Many,
many were homeless. The only advantage for the Zulu
impis was that they were completely mobile: they needed
no wagons, only boys who could run with them, carrying
cartridges and water. And what did that come to? King
Cetshwayo looked at his generals. Zibebu from the north
was not there. Dunn was with the enemy, showing them
ways into the country which he had said was his. The
King said heavily, "There is only one thing to do. We must
never fight a real battle, a battle of chest and horns; if we
do, they will kill us utterly. We must attack and run, attack and run, so that they will never know whether or
when the blow will strike. We will not look for a battlefield but for rough country, *dongas* and bush, where we
can be hidden."

There was a silence. "The King has spoken," said Dabulamanzi, his brother. "These were wise words."

"Yet it was chest and horns at Isandhlwana," said Tshingiswayo.

"They were not prepared. They did not go into *laager*.
Now they are prepared. Could you do the same today?"
And Tshingiswayo shook his head and said nothing.

But one of the younger *indunas* said, "The regiments
will stay together when there is hope of a battle with
glory. And also remembering all the good things we took
from the camp at Isandhlwana."

193

"Great riches!" said another. "Good killing!" And indeed he was wearing the red coat with gilt trappings and shining buttons of an English officer, though it did not meet around his chest.

"There will be no more riches," said Cetshwayo. "Only hard blows and perhaps death if we are to defend our own cattle and our own homes."

"Men must fight as they know," said another. "We know how to fight a battle. But not to hide."

And another, "My *impi* took many rifles at Isandhlwana —and many cartridges!"

"They will all be needed," said Tshingiswayo softly, "either way."

"To use or to surrender," said Dabulamanzi.

Another of the *indunas* cried out: "There is no regiment which will lay down its arms in front of the whites. Not one! The shame of it!" How many of the Usutu even, the King's men, would be loyal to this point? Cetshwayo looked around, into face after face, then turned away.

The Chief Councilor, Mnyamisna, said, almost despairingly: "But if that is the price for our country, it must be paid."

"Call on the young men and they will melt away," said another *induna*. "Like snow under the sun. Like water into the ground."

"If that is so," said Cetshwayo, "their officers die. Slowly. And also their commander."

"If men are found to carry the King's word," said the *induna* between his teeth.

Cetshwayo said: "Find me the Dutchman." Someone

slipped out to find the Dutch trader Vijn. They knew the King must want to write a letter. He signed to Mnya-misna: "Come."

The next day messengers came to Chelmsford, carrying two huge tusks of ivory, driving as many cattle as could be collected from the pest-stricken herds, saying that the field guns were being sent back but it was not in the King's power to surrender the arms. Cetshwayo had not wanted to send those tusks, which had hung so long on the wall of his house; they came from the time when there were still elephants in Zululand and when the authority of Shaka the great Zulu went far over the lands which the whites now held. But he wanted still less to see them back with a message that the conditions had not been complied with, though the surrender of any thousand warriors would do instead of a named *impi;* meanwhile, the British army would halt for a day. But at the end of the day there were still only promises.

And now the enemy was camped on the banks of the river almost opposite Ulundi, the King's kraal, and only a few miles away from it. The King's own place. So many houses! So many beautiful cattle! Already some of the women were hurrying away, carrying babies and bundles; nobody tried to stop them. Tears and anger.

The White Umfolozi was down, the drift easy to cross. But there was a Zulu regiment on the far side. Perhaps two. Not there to give up arms! Chelmsford's engineers built strong earthworks. But all at once they saw a herd of beautiful white oxen being driven toward them from the King's kraal. A peace offering!

195

And so it was. But the *impis* in front of the river were furious. These were the white oxen of the Zulu people, the oxen that Shaka had put aside and bred for their pure white skins, which made the most honored shields! No other people in Africa had oxen like these. The English must not have them. The young men turned the cattle and drove them back. Let the King not think he could give the best things in Zululand to the enemy!

There was no more answer to the peace terms. Cetshwayo had been overruled; the *indunas* had insisted on fighting. The next day there was a small battle with the English cavalry sent out to reconnoiter the ground around Ulundi. The cavalry withdrew. "Look!" said the *indunas*. "They are running." But Cetshwayo knew this was not so, and so did the older generals. The *impis* who had fought were feasting and singing, but tomorrow, not having taken his advice, they would be dead.

For the English army advanced in strength, the terrible artillery crashing and destroying from afar. The *impis* advanced with their old courage and spirit, but they were killed and killed. The few that were left were speared as they ran by the pursuing and delighted lancers. The royal kraal with its hundreds of houses went up in flames.

Cetshwayo could not look on it. He knew how it would be. He was no young warrior, but an aging man whose word had been disregarded. Whose country would now be taken by the whites as so many other countries had been. Whose nation was broken. He had left so as not to see. When the remains of the defeated army came to him, he tried to encourage them, telling them it was not too late to do what he had advised, to pursue and harass the English and make them see that the Zulu nation still lived. But most of them just melted away, throwing off their plumes and bracelets which they would never any longer be able to wear. Never. And the King, seeing this, fled.

Tshingiswayo and Mnyamisna were prisoners. The Dutchman Vijn had joined in the hunt, hoping for a reward. Perhaps also Dunn. Now the King must hide in the Bush, fewer and fewer of his people with him. Once or twice he could rest a few days in a friendly kraal, knowing at least that nobody would speak. Zulu men, women, and children were threatened, beaten, had their cattle taken and their homes burned, or were offered huge bribes, but said nothing. No more than the Highlanders after the '45 spoke of their hunted King.

But he was caught at last. He was completely exhausted. There was only a small party with him, a few oldish men and women. The interpreter on the hunt was the son of a Norwegian missionary who had been allowed to set up a mission in Zululand and who had been very friendly with the King. Cetshwayo looked at young Oftebro and said, "Was your father a friend of mine so long that you should do this to me?"

During the slow march back to Sir Garnet Wolseley's camp—for he had taken over from Chelmsford—three of the men and a woman tried to escape; two of the men were shot. The King marched on, his cloak over his shoulders, his royal staff in his hands, a big heavy man, pain not being allowed to show on his face. Sir Garnet told him that he was now deposed, his kingdom would be split up and divided and he himself was a prisoner for as long as Her Majesty the Queen cared to keep him.

Every week his captivity took him farther, first to the sea. He had never been in a boat, but he did not show the soldiers of his escort any trace of fear, which might have dimmed the respect they had learned for him. The boat took him to Cape Town and prison.

Meanwhile, Sir Garnet held a meeting at Ulundi with all the head chiefs of Zululand. They were told that the King would never return and their country would be divided up into thirteen districts, over each of which a chief would rule according to the wishes of the Natal government. He himself would nominate the chiefs. He did this without consulting Shepstone, who would at least have put in chiefs who were respected and might have kept order. Instead, Sir Garnet's nominees were all kinds of small men who now had the chance—as soon as the British left—of revenging themselves on all their old enemies and enriching themselves. Zibebu in the north, always doubtfully loyal to the King, had a large district, but the largest of all went to John Dunn. The disputed territory was allocated to the Boers, who by now had decided firmly to be independent again.

A British Resident was appointed, but with only a small police force; he was unable to stop the civil wars which now flared up. The King's brothers and his heir, young Dinuzulu, were put under Zibebu, who took their cattle and made them work as servants. This shocked many of the Zulu people, but they were next put under Dunn, who treated them even worse, unable to forgive those who, because they had been so generous to him, had given him the bad conscience which now he must live with.

After a few months of fighting here and there, injustice and unease, petitions and deputations began to come to Natal, asking for the return of the King. But it was two years later that a meeting was called, in an attempt to get a settlement and meet the complaints about the tyranny of Dunn, Zibebu, and another appointed chief, Uhamu, a man who had surrendered early in the war and so got into favor. Now a Hut Tax was proposed, to pay for police, roads, the Resident, and so on; it would have been more honest to take over completely, but might have looked less well in England.

How much of this did the imprisoned King hear? Probably plenty, for he had many visitors, though some came to look as though he were a strange animal in a zoo. But Harriette Colenso wrote to him in Zulu. She knew all his supporters, and her mother says, "She is too much absorbed in her conversations with her black visitors to be able to attend to much else." The King now had an interpreter whose father had been one of the missionaries who stayed many years in Zululand. This young man helped him to appeal to England. Somehow, Cetshwayo thought, if he could see the Queen of England, everything would come right. Two royals would understand one another. Deep would speak to deep.

So he was sent to England. He may well have been anxious, even afraid. But he was a London showpiece. Everyone was very kind, including the Queen, who gave him a quarter of an hour interview and lunch at Osborne, as well as a silver cup and the usual signed photograph. The English in their days of power were always ready to be kind to those they had conquered. Cetshwayo emerged from the

vast bosom of London having agreed to go back to a de-
militarized Zululand with a part—and this was left vague
—reserved for those who did not wish to be ruled by him.
He only protested about Dunn, this adventurer whom he
had befriended, giving him cattle and wives, this man
whom he had loved as a brother but who had persecuted
his children and friends. But nobody in England paid
much attention, and the Natal authorities were doing their
best to make things difficult and stop his return. It was
odd that so many of the King's friends in England were
liberals, Republicans even, who hated the imperialist
spread but would have found the devotion of a people to
their autocratic King just a bit out of date.

He landed again at the Cape and waited anxiously to go
back. Weeks and months passed. There was fighting again,
with Dunn trying hard to be made paramount chief; however, he was also acting as adviser to Zibebu, Cetshwayo's
bitterest enemy. It is clear that most Zulus quite simply
wanted their King back. But more and more conditions
were made. Cetshwayo protested that these were new; the
Queen in England had not made them.

In the end he signed and was taken to a small port, land-
ing from an open boat wet through, probably to the
amusement of the sailors. Somsteu was there to greet him
and doubtless the King was glad to see him, hoping that
here was somebody who would understand the impossibil-
ity of a stable Zululand under the new conditions, with a
third in the north going to Zibebu and another third in the
south, including some of the best land, going to Natal but
with many of his people living in it. Meanwhile, his people
were being kept from him. "Every effort was made to take

the gloss off the affair," says Frances Colenso, and then she writes of "the Governor of this Colony doing everything in his power to hinder the King's return as if he had a personal hostility to him."

At the Installation many of the chiefs, especially his brother Dabulamanzi, protested at the new conditions, telling Shepstone that he was still "killing the King." But it was all useless. Zibebu had been confirmed in his chieftainship over all northern Zululand, and Dunn, angry at now being under the British Resident and losing his income as a government-appointed chief, was trying to make trouble in the hope of bettering himself. There were more and more quarrels, cattle raiding, and house burning. The King no longer had his old powers; he could not stop it. Suddenly it burst into civil war. His party, the Usutu, were badly disciplined; there had been no military training or drill allowed; it was all a mob. Zibebu's army dodged the combined Usutu forces, swept down on Ulundi, massacred everyone, and burned all the houses. Cetshwayo was there but fled out of the burning into a clump of trees.

Was it a Zulu who lifted his spear against the King and wounded him in the thigh? People say it was an outsider, one of the young thugs who had joined up with Zibebu. Badly wounded, he took refuge with a few of his oldest followers at the kraal of a small chief who had been one of Shaka's soldiers many years before. Later he was persuaded to move to another kraal. And here, a few months later, he died. While he was still a fugitive he was visited by a young English reporter who had the courage to tell the truth and publish it.

His body in a huge coffin was taken to the chosen grave in the Nkhandhla forest; after the burial the wagon was dismantled and all its pieces piled onto the grave. No doubt the iron rims of the wagon wheels, the axle and brake, the nuts and bolts are still lying there, still guarded, as King Cetshwayo's memory is guarded in the hearts of thousands of Zulus.

Epilogue

This was the end of independent Zululand. Afterward, there were what British and Boers alike called Zulu rebellions. People who have had all they lived for taken from them, or about to be taken, fight hard and without regard to the rules of "civilized" warfare. Later they acquiesced; some went to other parts of Africa. They looked for other ways of getting themselves freedom and satisfactions of a different kind. Yet they also remembered; they know themselves still. When a Zulu becomes, say, a doctor, a great teacher or lawyer or scientist, a singer or painter, or a freedom fighter, that is felt as an honor to all the dispersed nation.

This awareness of identity survives and gives people something to be proud of, but, as different tribes and nations begin to know themselves not only as separate but, more important, as a whole, as Africans, they begin to think of themselves differently. They are looking at a future of a new kind when they will no longer be taking orders from people of another color and obeying blindly just because they themselves were born brown or black. They are looking at a future when they will be counted everywhere as full human beings, to be respected as such, to be treated as fellow workers and colleagues.

But people who look at a future must do so from knowledge of the past. They must have their feet on the ground. Africans are finding inspiration from their own great figures. Sometimes this inspiration may lead them into attitudes which may seem strange and unreasonable to non-Africans, firmly sticking to their own past, but not to those, like the Colenso family in the story of Cetshwayo, who start from real sympathy and knowledge that brotherhood not only makes economic sense but makes everyone happy.

Let me quote here from the speech made by Nelson Rolihlahla Mandela at the Rivonia trial in which he and others were accused of treason against the South African government. He is the son of a chief and was brought up in the country, herding goats like other little boys. "In my youth in the Transkei I listened to the elders of my tribe telling stories of the old days. Among the tales they related to me were those of wars fought by our ancestors in defense of the Fatherland. The names of Dingaan and Bampata, Hintsa and Makana, Squngthi and Dalasile, Moshesh and Sekukuni, were praised as the glory of the entire African nation. I hoped then that my life might offer me the opportunity to serve my people and make my own humble contribution to their freedom struggle."

His hopes were realized fully. He made his contribution, perhaps still makes it wherever and whenever he is remembered: that is often. He was one of the founders of Umkonto We Sizwe, the Spear of the Nation, an organization which was started in the Republic of South Africa when it was found that all legal methods of protest and opposition there to the principle of White supremacy had been closed to Africans. Either they accepted permanent inferiority or they had to break the laws. Throughout history, bad laws have had to be broken by brave men and women. Umkonto aimed at sabotage of the economic life of South Africa and of government buildings, but strictly without injuring or killing the people who had made and were enjoying the bad laws. Above all, Nelson Mandela and his friends did not want a black and white civil war. Because he and other leaders are in prison, this terrible war has become more likely.

You who have read this book will know some of the stories which young Nelson Mandela heard around the fire after he had brought in the goats, before he went to the city and the University of Witwatersrand—for that was still possible even in his time, though now the intelligent African boy or girl goes to a "Bantu University," which will not give him admittance to the professions, which are kept for whites only. You must judge for yourselves what kind of people the tellers and hearers of these stories are. You must judge for yourselves.